Getting to Know the Vietnamese
and Their Culture

Getting to Know the Vietnamese and Their Culture

Vuong G. Thuy, Ph.D.

FREDERICK UNGAR PUBLISHING CO.
NEW YORK

Library of Congress Cataloging in Publication Data

Vương Gia Thụy.
  Getting to know the Vietnamese and their culture.

  Bibliography: p.
  1. Vietnam—Civilization. I. Title.
DS556.42.V82   959.7   76-15659
ISBN 0-8044-0672-3
ISBN 0-8044-6905-9 pbk.

Note about the Author

Vuong G. Thuy is a language and culture specialist who now lives in New York City. Born in Vietnam, educated there and in Great Britain, he has his Ph.D. in linguistics from the Sorbonne in Paris. A teacher, newswriter, and editor in Saigon and London, he has taught at Cornell University and is the author of *Vietnamese in a Nutshell, Your New Country*, a bilingual guide to life in the United States, and of books on American English for Vietnamese.

President of Vietnam House, a nonprofit organization in New York, he is a consultant in the Vietnamese program for the New York City Board of Education. Dr. Thuy also conducts workshops and conferences throughout the country for teachers and administrators involved in primary, high school, and adult education who seek guidance in dealing with their new Indo-Chinese students.

Contents

Acknowledgments

May I express my most sincere gratitude to:

1. Professor David Cooper of Hunter College, New York City, who spent two years in Vietnam as a visiting Fulbright professor at the University of Saigon, Vietnam;

2. Mr. Christopher Howard, a newspaperman with working experience in Vietnam;

3. Ms. Milena Jovanovitch, a New York City reporter, who has been covering the resettlement of the Vietnamese refugees in the Greater New York area.

My appreciation to all of them for kindly offering to read the manuscript and for their valuable comments and suggestions.

I would also like to express my thanks to Ms. Nguyen Kim Hong, a Vietnamese educator with many years of teaching experience and a former classmate of mine, for reading, commenting on, and typing the manuscript.

Last, but not least, I would like to add that without the arrival of my compatriot evacuees in the United States, I would not have been motivated enough to write this book.

To all of them, I am very grateful.

VUONG G. THUY

Introduction

Recent resettlement efforts involving Vietnamese refugees have been frequently marked by sponsorship break-ups, misunderstandings caused by the seeming insensitivity of American friends, both agencies and individuals, and difficulties attendant upon the influx of Vietnamese students into American schools.

What is involved here is a twofold fact of life: a "culture shock" for the newcomers on the one hand, and a lack of understanding of Vietnamese cultural and social institutions on the other. These two seemingly opposite aspects of the same overall problem, that of smooth resettlement, are actually intertwined and account for most of the failures. No success can be achieved if either one is ignored.

The impact of the inevitable culture shock on refugees is aggravated by the fact that there is no established Vietnamese community in America. Whereas Cubans, for example, arrived in American cities to find neighborhoods where their native language was spoken and customs observed, Vietnamese are hampered in finding help because they lack this essential base.

This book is not intended as a panacea for all of the resettlement problems. It is a modest attempt to present some general information about Vietnamese cultural and social characteristics, and about the factors which have shaped those

1

characteristics, in the hope that it will be useful to those who have been helping Vietnamese refugees. For the sake of convenience, and as an acknowledgment of the ties of culture that still link the Vietnamese to their homeland, some of the text describing the background of Vietnamese life and attitudes is written in the present tense—a recollection of a way of life that may no longer exist.

We all hope that the newcomers will gradually overcome the culture shock through daily contact with their American fellows and through their "struggle for survival." Much-needed literature, workshops, and seminars (in Vietnamese) in dealing with the American way of life will also accelerate and facilitate the resettlement of these people. Because this book may also be used by Vietnamese speakers—in seminars and discussion groups, for example—it was thought useful to include a minimum number of phrases in Vietnamese as well as English. These will also be helpful to English speakers who may wish to learn certain simple phrases or forms of address in Vietnamese.

From the time the first Vietnamese refugees left the refugee camps in the United States to begin a new life, this author has been actively involved, both as a private citizen and later as a founder and president of Vietnam House in New York. Vietnam House is a nonprofit organization run by members of the Vietnamese community in this country to help about 6,000 refugees in their resettlement in the Greater New York area: New York City and neighboring New Jersey and Connecticut. This involvement has given him firsthand experience of the acuteness of the problems facing the refugees and their sponsors, as well as individuals and agencies working with them. It is his belief that the difficulties found in the Greater New York area may also surface elsewhere in the United States as long as the new residents are unable to stand on their own feet or fully adjust to a largely alien world.

As a Vietnamese-born resident of the United States for nine years, one with a variety of educational and teaching experience in Vietnam, Great Britain, France, and the United States, the author was able to foresee a great number of diversified problems facing the resettlement of the Vietnamese. It is his sincere hope that this book will contribute modestly to the overall effort by those who are involved in this worthwhile cause.

About the Vietnamese and Their Culture

They are, first of all, a proud people who claim to be descendants of a dragon and an angel, with four thousand years of civilization and culture colored by a glorified history of repeated and successful fighting against foreign invasions, right up to modern times. Many important and complex factors have shaped the thinking and behavior of the Vietnamese. Even some Vietnamese admit that the behavioral complexity of their fellow countrymen is often bewildering. An awareness of the factors which have shaped Vietnamese thinking, behavior, and cultural characteristics is vital to any attempt to understand the Vietnamese, especially those newly arrived on American soil. These factors can be classified into four broad categories: culturé, values, characteristics, and education.

I

Cultural Background

Religion and religious philosophies have played a very important role in influencing the Vietnamese culture.

1. Buddhism (563–483 B.C.)

In Vietnam, Buddhism is the predominant religion. An estimated 90 percent of the population are Buddhist. Buddhism was introduced to the Vietnamese in its early days. Despite its ups and downs throughout the history of Vietnam, Buddhism has set a very deep imprint on the thinking and behavior of the Vietnamese. This religion was originated by an Indian prince, Siddhartha, later called Gautama Buddha. Buddha means "the Enlightened One." In 534 B.C., the prince, for the first time in his life, saw a sick man, an old man, a holy man, and a dead man. Afterward he wandered aimlessly for six years and then meditated for forty-nine days under a Bodhi tree at Gaya in Magadha. He achieved Nirvana or *Enlightenment* and taught *Salvation* in Bihar, West of Bengal, until he died at the age of eighty. Buddha formulated these Four Noble Truths:

1. Man was born to suffer, and he suffers from one life to the next.

2. *Craving* is the cause of suffering: craving for pleasure, possessions, and cessation of pain.
3. The cure for craving is nonattachment to all things including self.
4. To achieve nonattachment one must take the eightfold path of right conduct, right effort, right intentions, right livelihood, right meditations, right mindfulness, right speech, and right views.

Divine judgment or messianic expectation does not exist in Buddhism since there is no provision for God in this religion. On the other hand, dharma or the law of cause and effect determines an individual's fate or destiny.

Buddhist monks and nuns practice celibacy, nonviolence, poverty and vegetarianism.

There are two main branches of Buddhism: Mahayana or Greater Vehicle, which can be found in North Vietnam and certain areas in Central Vietnam, and Hinayana or Lesser Vehicle, which has been practiced mainly in South Vietnam and in a few regions to the north of South Vietnam. According to Mahayana, laymen as well as Buddhist monks and nuns may attain the highest ideal of Bodhisattva, the enlightened one who liberates himself by personal sacrifice, while Hinayana holds that only their monks and nuns may attain Nirvana, the Enlightenment.

2. Confucianism (551–479 B.C.)

The second striking influence on culture and human development in Vietnam is Confucianism. Misconstrued as a religion, it is better described as a religious philosophy or Code of Social Behavior than as a religion in the accepted sense, since

Confucianism has no church or clergy and is in no way an institution like Buddhism or other religions. In fact, Confucianism or Confucianist teaching was not advocated by Confucius alone, but rather by the group of Ju, or meek ones, of which he was a member. Confucius' real name was K'ung Futzo or Master Kung. For some time he worked as a keeper of accounts in the province of Lu and later he became the first and most prominent teacher in Chinese history, instructing people of all walks of life in the six arts: ceremonies, music, archery, charioteering, history, and numbers.

Confucius strongly advocated humanism, which involves devotion to human interests. In Confucianism, the main ethics are Jen (benevolence or humanity) and Shu (tolerance or reciprocity). Confucius stressed personal or self cultivation, the basis of which is filial piety, an obligation that, along with altruism, was strongly emphasized in his teachings. The Great Master's Mid Path denotes the spirit of compromise and avoidance of extreme actions. He also pointed out that truth involves knowledge of one's own faults and that man could be led by the example of his own time or by the example of the past. He therefore advocated worship of heaven, and revered ancestors and great men, but he did not advocate prayer because he insisted that man should control his own destiny.

Throughout his life, Confucius was always preoccupied by rituals and music. He attributed the chaotic situation and social ills of his lifetime to the neglect or abuse of rites and ceremonies by the rulers of his country. He strongly believed that social and family order could be attained by music, adherence to proper social rites, and respect for authority, all of which he believed essential for the maintenance of social and family order. In other words, rank within the family (in terms of age and relationship) should be strictly observed, and within the social hierarchy one has to respect and obey the king (quân), teacher (sư) and father (phụ) in that order of priority. Therefore, an individual's relationship vis-à-vis others must be clearly spelled out by specific and nonambiguous terms of address.

3. Taoism (600–500 B.C.)

Another very important source of influence is Taoism, founded by Lao-tzu or Lao-tze or Lao-tse, the famed Chinese philosopher. According to Lao-tzu, Tao or the Ultimate and Unconditioned Being could be attained by the practice of thrift, humility, and compassion. Taoism is characterized by a belief in numerous gods although Lao-tzu himself did not permit this, and by superstitions. Taoism also stresses man's life and the nature of man. The principal teachings of Taoism are charity, simplicity, patience, contentment, and harmony between man and man, and harmony between man and nature. In the interest of harmony, all forms of confrontation should be avoided. On the other hand, naturalism—a belief that all truths are derived from nature and natural causes—was also strongly advocated and as a consequence Taoism is against regulations or organization of any kind. Another characteristic of Taoism is its acceptance of the worship of deities of other religions, although this practice is limited to certain Taoist groups only. Contrary to Confucianism but like Buddhism, this philosophical religion does have clergy and temples, the chief of which is the White Cloud Temple in Peking. In Vietnam, although the Taoist clergy is practically nonexistent or at least not obvious, the Taoist teaching has been passed on from one generation to another through literature, books, education, and traditional practice. It has a strong hold over Vietnamese thinking and culture, as well as the Vietnamese way of life.

4. Christianity

Roman Catholicism was introduced into Vietnam in the late sixteenth century by European missionaries, first by Portuguese, then Spanish, later French. This new religion flourished particularly in the seventeenth and eighteenth centuries but suffered persecutions and suppressions during the nineteenth century. Roman Catholicism prospered again during French rule in Vietnam from the late nineteenth century to 1954, when French troops were forced to withdraw from Vietnam after their military defeat at Dien Bien Phu. At present Catholicism has an estimated two million followers. Although Catholic followers represent only a small percentage of the total population of about 17 million in South Vietnam, the Catholic Church is one of the best organized educational and religious forces. Vietnamese Catholics have, by and large, played a very important role in the cultural and political life of Vietnam. Although Catholicism is not as widespread nor has it been practiced as long as Buddhism, Confucianism, or Taoism, its influence on the Vietnamese way of life cannot be ignored. The practice and influence of other branches of Christianity, such as Protestantism, have been very limited.

5. Religious Sects and Animism

It should be noted that there are also some other religious sects, such as Cao Dai (practicing a combination of religion and the worship of outstanding men in the world), and Hoa

Hao (a Buddhist sect). These religious sects have been confined to very limited regions in South Vietnam and their influence on Vietnamese culture is minimal.

Last, but not least, is the fact that not only do the Vietnamese practice and believe in the religious and philosophical teachings described above, but they also believe in the existence of spirits or animism. They are superstitious and are afraid of the spirits and natural forces. They worship many spirits such as the spirit of an old tree, a kitchen, a dark cave, a mountain and the dead. They also believe in astrology, fortune telling, omens and the meanings of natural signs. This belief and practice have been widespread among the rural population and to some extent the urban people of all social classes. For example, when you step out of your house for the first time in the day and if the first person you pass by is a female, it is a bad sign for the whole day, but if the person is a male everything you do during the day will work out smoothly and in your favor. If you own a store and business is slow, you may burn a piece of paper to chase away the evil spirit which has been preventing your customers from doing business with you. Belief in astrology may prevent you from going into a business venture on a certain day if the lunar calendar indicates that that day is not good for it. These are some examples of how different beliefs can deeply influence an individual's daily behavior.

By and large, the Vietnamese do not follow one religion only, but a mixture of religions and religious philosophies. If a Vietnamese is a Buddhist, he not only practices Buddhism but also observes Confucian rituals and Taoist teachings, or may even strongly believe in animism. A Catholic might worship his ancestors and believe in the existence of spirits.

These religious and philosophical influences are unmistakably reflected in Vietnamese literature[1] and education.

6. Nonreligious Factors

A number of nonreligious and nonphilosophical events have also tremendously affected the Vietnamese people. Constant warfare from the beginning of their history is one example. The two recent long and devastating wars with the resulting displacement of the population have altered or destroyed to some extent (depending on individual experience) many of the Vietnamese characteristics and values. Political instability and the introduction of foreign political ideologies, Western technology, and civilization have also contributed to the process of change in terms of traditional values and culture.

[1] See the "Story of Lady Kieu" by William Negherban, *Some Aspects of Vietnamese Culture,* Center for Vietnamese Studies, Southern Illinois University, Carbondale, Illinois, 1972, pp. 39-58.

5

II

Vietnamese Values

The Vietnamese system of values does not place a great emphasis on material well-being or monetary success per se. In the Vietnamese tradition, hard work, wealth, and possessions are recognized as merits, not values as such.

Rather, the values which are highly esteemed are based on four broad categories of considerations: spirituality, education, family, and humanism. Spiritual considerations have been strongly emphasized from one generation to another, not only in books or through formal education but in family education and everyday life contacts as well. They represent a spectrum of good acts and virtues. Sacrifice and self-sacrifice of all forms (spiritual, emotional, physical, and material) for others and especially for legitimate rulers are highly valued and recognized.

One is taught to forget oneself. In other words, the self is supposed to be secondary in anyone's considerations.

This category of values also encompasses modesty and humility and embraces acts of goodness such as straightforwardness and the keeping of promises. Breaking a promise, however unimportant it may seem to be, is considered a serious violation of social expectations and usually leads to certain unfavorable consequences because the Vietnamese people usually take such a break seriously. Virtues, widely recognized as values, are numerous and range from merited traits such as loyalty, patience, strict morality, and stamina, to seemingly old-fashioned ideals such as virginity and faithfulness, including faithful widowhood.[1] Today, for some Vietnamese, especially the young, urban and/or the well-educated, the last two values, namely virginity and faithfulness, may no longer retain their power.

A second type of values is established on the basis of education. The Vietnamese, by and large, have the highest esteem for education whether they are rich or poor, educated or illiterate, urban or rural, sophisticated or unsophisticated. Traditionally, learning and knowledge are held in great respect, and education has always been one of the main concerns of Vietnamese parents. As a consequence, Vietnamese teachers have been highly respected not only by students, young and old, but by their parents and by most citizens. There are many reasons for this respect. For one thing, socio-political conditions have generally made education the surest and easiest way for people of all ranks to climb up the social ladder. For another, since a European-style aristocratic system based mainly on land ownership or heredity did not exist in the history of Vietnam, educational achievement measured by examination has been the main criterion for recruitment and social advancement. Thus, people of the humblest origin could, through education, hold very high positions and be well respected. This

---

[1] The phrase *faithful widowhood* implies that the living spouse stays faithful to the dead husband or wife without remarrying or engaging in any sexual acts with anybody. Generally speaking, faithful widowhood is, rightly or wrongly, strongly expected of the widow more than of the widower, especially when she has young children to raise.

gives rise to concern for status more than wealth. Men of accumulated wealth lacking a good education or proper conduct are, generally speaking, not highly regarded and in some extreme cases are even despised. An individual's education also determines, to a great extent, his social class as well as his self-esteem.

But perhaps the most important factor of all in the Vietnamese value system remains the family. For the majority of Vietnamese, the family is the center of an individual's life. Not only do the Vietnamese feel deeply attached to their families, but they are also extremely concerned with their family's welfare, growth, harmony, pride, prestige, reputation, honor, filial piety, etc. The family claims first allegiance.

Family loyalty plays a very important role in the conduct of members of the family. Family identity can be a tremendous source of pride or dishonor. The duty and responsibility of each member of the family toward his family and those of his family toward himself are tightly interlocked and inseparable. Family loyalty among the Vietnamese has engendered a strong sense of duty and responsibility. Each child is taught to carry out these two obligations in order to pay off the debt of birth and rearing by the parents. Accordingly, his duty and responsibility, although taken for granted in most cases, are generally carried out quite seriously. A violation of social and moral codes can seriously damage or destroy one's growth or acceptance in the community. A behavioral deviation by a Vietnamese might not only hurt him, but also his family. If an unmarried girl becomes pregnant, for instance, it could result in unbearable shame or dishonor and create heavy social pressures on her and her family. If no satisfactory solution can be found, she might either no longer be recognized by her family or would even have to leave her family and native village for some distant place where her identity would be unknown to the people around her. In some extreme cases, it can result in suicide or even forced suicide. A socially unmatched marriage or the living together of two unmarried persons is usually not acceptable and can cause serious disappointment or humiliation for the families concerned. Desertion by anyone in the family can badly hurt the family reputation and all efforts, not surprisingly, will be made to mask this "shameful" act. For Americans, all this may sound as if the Vietnamese people were still living in Victorian times, but many practices which are common or socially acceptable in American society would be considered serious deviations from social norms in Vietnam.

It would not be uncommon to find paid public announcements in newspapers indicating that Mr. and Mrs. so-and-so no longer recognize their ill-behaved child, or that Mr. X does not wish to recognize his deserting wife any longer and will not be responsible for whatever act she might be engaged in, or something of that nature. On the other hand, the successful completion of a difficult or competitive examination can boost family pride and prestige tremendously; and of course, such good news should be spread as quickly and as widely as possible. This is, again, a good illustration of how important a role education plays in Vietnamese society. If it is necessary, a Vietnamese will proudly and readily forget himself by sacrificing even his future or such desirable things as love, even physical existence, as the case may be, for the sake of his family's welfare or harmony. Filial piety, the most important and essential virtue advocated by Confucius, dictates that the Vietnamese think of their parents first, even at their own expense. A young girl might therefore give up her education (which may be very important for her future), delay her marriage, or abandon her love altogether to be able to take care of her younger siblings and elderly mother. It is not unusual to hear of a young husband who, just for the sake of filial piety, has had to ignore or abandon his young wife to please his mother because the latter did not like or could not get along with the wife. The husband's mother (mẹ chồng) in Vietnam has often been known to be unreasonably strict with her young daughters-in-law. There is a famous comparison, "as strict as the husband's mother." This type of filial piety is sometimes taken very seriously, to the point of making no sense. Behavior of all these kinds is not uncommon in Vietnam and clearly demonstrates how the Vietnamese conceive of filial piety, and of their duty and responsibility toward their family.

Not only are the Vietnamese deeply attached to their family, they are also strongly attached to their land, native village, ancestors' tombs, etc. Traditionally, there is great respect for ancestors' spirits and achievements. Because of all these strong emotional attachments, Vietnamese usually do not wish to leave their villages or home towns. Many of them never even cross the village borderline in their lifetime. This is one of the main reasons why immobility is a Vietnamese characteristic in contrast with the dynamic and constant mobility of Americans. The Vietnamese revere their ancestors as "sacred," and because of this great respect for ancestors, the Vietnamese have developed a sense of respect for the elderly. For the Vietnamese, age is wisdom and deserves high esteem. As a consequence, elderly people are accorded the highest standing in society and in the family. At the dining table, the younger people show their respect for the older people by waiting until the latter start eating first, and then, during the meal, by serving them.

Any insult to the ancestors of a Vietnamese or to a respected older person is, as a rule, taken very seriously and sometimes leads to damaging and irreparable consequences. Thus, the most serious insults in Vietnamese can literally be translated into English as something like "Your father!," "Your mother!," "Your ancestors!". . .

Last but not least, the Vietnamese value system is traditionally based on humanism rather than on materialism. Human factors are highly valued and stressed. Humanism, strongly advocated by Confucian teachings, offers important and valuable guidance for the philosophy of life and everyday acts of the Vietnamese. It is, therefore, also one of the three fundamental principles of education in Vietnam.[2]

1. The Vietnamese Family

The family in Vietnam is an extended one, unlike the typical family in the United States, which normally consists of the father, mother, and unmarried children. The Vietnamese family is composed of the parents, all children, and their in-laws, the grandparents (paternal as well as maternal), the great-grandparents, and also in some circumstances, uncles and aunts and their spouses, cousins, grandchildren, great-grandchildren, and all in-laws. In other words, it might embrace up to six generations, with everybody who is related either by blood or marriage. There is always a strong feeling of attachment between the members of the same family in spite of the generation gap, which can be large or small.

The center for the family is a house which does not necessarily accommodate everybody. The availability of living space determines the size of the family living together. But typically, one finds grandparents, father, mother, children, and grandchildren living under the same roof. Although not all members

---

[2] See also p. 62.

of the extended family are housed together, they tend to cluster around a certain area such as a village, small town, or places of easy access in large cities.

The Vietnamese are inclined to develop a feeling of isolation or loneliness if their relatives or friends are not around them. It is very important for them to be close to these people, especially when they find themselves living in a totally alien world.

As a social institution, the Vietnamese family or home is a source of wonder for some Westerners. Not only is it the backbone of Vietnamese society, it is also a socially self-sufficient and autonomous unit. In a way, it is a mini-commune where its members live and share together, a maternity center where children are born (especially in rural areas), a funeral home where funeral rituals are performed, a religious place where the family altar is set up to revere ancestors or observe religious rituals, an adoption agency where adoption by a relative is arranged, an orphanage where orphans are brought up and given love and affection (adoption in its ordinary sense is very rare in Vietnam), a courtroom where conflicts or disputes between members are settled, a welfare center where assistance and social security services are rendered, a hospital where patients are treated, a nursing home where the elderly are taken good care of,[3] an educational institution where family and formal education is provided, a bank where money is available, a council where all important decisions affecting one or more than one family member are made and carried out,

---

[3] Because of all this, the concept of welfare assistance and social services in the United States is totally unfamiliar to Vietnamese newcomers. It is difficult for them, at least at this stage, fully to understand how American people look at this type of assistance.

and a place where all members share the joys, the sadness, the enjoyments, the suffering of life.

Family continuity is accorded highest consideration, and for a family without boys there is sadness and serious concern. It is not unusual for parents, seeing that the only son has no chance of having male heirs to carry on the family's name, to try, and if necessary, to succeed in exercising tremendous pressure on a son and daughter in-law to find another woman for their son, even at the risk of creating a family rupture.

The Vietnamese family has been so indispensable for the existence and survival of Vietnamese society and of the nation that it has been said without exaggeration that if anyone wishes to destroy that society or nation, he must first destroy the Vietnamese family.

2. The Vietnamese Man

According to Confucian teaching, to be a man one must take four important steps: he must first know how to cultivate himself (Tu Thân); then he must govern or run his own family properly (Tề Gia); without these two prerequisites he might not be able to rule the country (Trị Quốc); and only after fulfillment of the three above required steps might he pacify the whole world (Bình Thiên Hạ).

In order to achieve the first step of self-cultivation, he must meet five requirements: 1) he must be merciful, kind, benevolent, and human (Nhân); 2) he must adhere to rites and ceremonies and strictly observe the family and social hierarchies (Lễ); 3) he must help the needy and desperate (Nghĩa); 4) he must have strong will power and determination (Chí); and 5) he should be consistent and loyal so that people can trust and have confidence in him (Tín).

Despite the recent importation of Western-style ways of life and current feminist movements, including the Women's Liberation Movement in the United States, the Vietnamese man, or more accurately the husband, is still the "boss" (if not the "big boss" any more), or at least he claims to be. In normal and traditional conditions, he is the breadwinner and decision-maker for his family. He is supposedly the most important member of the family and definitely has a higher status than his wife.

He goes out to work to make money, but he hands over to his wife whatever he makes so that she can buy food and pay bills. He is usually content with whatever pocket money his wife gives him. It is inconceivable for the husband and wife to have separate bank accounts or properties.[4]

While the husband helps his wife do heavy or menial work, he will not step in the kitchen to take over the cooking. He expects his wife and older children to serve him at home after a long and hard working day in the office. When he comes home, he educates his children or at least helps them with their homework if such help is necessary. Along with his wife, he is responsible for providing an education for his children at home as well as at school and any help they may need. Responsibility for children does not necessarily end when they marry. It is quite common for parents to support their married children financially for quite a long time after their marriage.

The father is an authority figure and will not hesitate to discipline his children even by physical means if necessary. Although he can do whatever he wants, his sincere desire for

[4] In Vietnam only a handful of big businessmen and businesswomen are familiar with banking services. The majority of the Vietnamese people have never stepped into a bank, let alone know how to use these services.

family harmony and his fear of hurting his family's image usually and effectively prevents him from abusive or damaging acts.

When decisions must be made regarding important issues such as the marriage of his children, he usually consults not only his wife and the children concerned but also other members of his family, such as his parents, his parents-in-law, his brothers and sisters, his uncles and aunts, etc. But the final decision is still his, and appropriate actions are taken.

This picture of a typical Vietnamese man has a number of elements of the typical "good husband" in America, but the differences lie in the fact that the Vietnamese man's "authority" and responsibility vis-à-vis his wife and children are much more institutionalized, recognized, and vigorously exercised without much resistance. Besides, they have been traditionally taken for granted. There are many reasons for all of this, which we will explore in the section below when we attempt to analyze the Vietnamese woman's role at home and in society. Remember that the Vietnamese man is the one you must talk to in any dealings with his family if you want to get things done.

3. The Vietnamese Woman

Vietnamese women are highly regarded by Westerners, who find them very graceful and gentle with all sorts of qualities that men look for. There is, in fact, some truth in the popular though rather exaggerated saying in Vietnam that "the husband is king and his wife is his slave." Generally speaking, Vietnamese women have been considered subordinate to men and are treated as secondary to their husbands in every respect.

Vietnamese women have been traditionally accorded a very

limited social life and low standing in society. As young girls, they are expected to keep their virginity until they get married and to get married only once in their life. On top of this, as married women, they are expected to respect and be faithful to their husbands and accept whatever fate might come. When a woman gets married, she is no longer considered to belong to her family but becomes a member of her husband's family. In other words, she is assumed to have a new duty and responsibility toward her husband and in-laws only. The facts, however, are sometimes different. Many married women still feel strongly about their own parents and relatives. Their love for, and responsibility toward their relatives often overshadows their married lives and new responsibilities.

Our women are taught to observe three basic practices: while they are still under their parents' protection, they must be obedient to their fathers (tại gia tōng phụ); when they get married, they have to be submissive to their husbands (xuất giá tōng phu); and when their husbands die, they must listen to their grown-up sons (phu tử tōng tử). This kind of teaching is clearly reflected in the fact that most Vietnamese women are very shy, often lack self-confidence, and are anything but aggressive. Women's beauty is usually more highly praised in terms of virtues than in physical attributes. Under the old custom a good woman must have four feminine virtues: 1) she must be good at housework, needlework, or any work peculiar to women (Công); 2) she must have feminine deportment and appearance (Dung); 3) she must speak gently and be careful with her speech (Ngôn); and 4) she must show good conduct and act in a virtuous way (Hạnh).

The role of women has traditionally been confined to the home. They are expected to bring up and educate their children, take care of the household, and not only serve their husbands in every respect, but also their husbands' families as well. They are expected to sacrifice themselves for their husbands and children.

Women without male heirs are traditionally disgraced and in some cases abandoned by their husbands' families. The majority of them are basically housewives and home-oriented. They stay home and do not go out to work. Even though in rural areas women generally do go out to the rice paddy fields to work with their husbands, they are still fully responsible for their households and families. Because of this role, the old conception strongly held that women had no need for education, or at least higher education, and should not acquire more than sufficient reading and writing skills plus the four basic arithmetic operations. Of course, in primary or junior high schools they also take other courses such as history, geography, sanitation (hygiene), civic instruction, etc. but very often they do not go beyond basic knowledge.

Career women were unheard of or were very rare until recently. Although there are now some career women, they represent only a very small percentage of the work force, and very few women have reached leadership positions or attained important powers. Traditionally, Vietnamese women have a very limited education and must live up to all sorts of expectations from society and their males. They lack social mobility and depend economically on their husbands and thus do not enjoy the freedom of their American counterparts. Furthermore, the social, educational, economic, and political set-up in Vietnam has traditionally prevented Vietnamese women from gaining a status in any way equal to that of Vietnamese men. Vietnamese women are legally incompetent. They cannot sell property, make any important deals, or sign any legal documents without their husbands' consent or permission.

The Vietnamese woman keeps her maiden name even after marriage, but she usually uses her husband's given name preceded by Bà "Mrs." to address herself to others. For example:

Her maiden name: Vương Thị Phúc
                      (Fam./Mid./Given)

Her husband's name: Trịnh Đức Thịnh
                      (Fam./Mid./Given)

She will be addressed as Mrs. Thịnh while retaining her own name Vương Thị Phúc. Sometimes she is addressed even as Mrs. Phúc. If she is a businesswoman or professional, she would tend to use her own name, in this case Vương Thị Phúc, to conduct business.

Despite their limited rights and secondary place in the family, the role of Vietnamese women in both the family and the general society should not be underestimated. They often exercise great control over their husbands, their home, and the family purse, for one thing; for another, Vietnam's long history of nearly constant warfare has often left commerce largely in the hands of women, who have proven themselves competent when their competence is needed. They have become accustomed to being on their own, making money and taking care of the family and household while their men are missing or fighting somewhere on the battlefields. They frequently make decisions for their families while their men concern themselves with making money or other activities outside the home. Some of them influence their husbands even in traditionally masculine domains such as politics. There have been numerous circumstances in our history when women in fact ruled the country themselves or by working through their husbands. It was well known that favors or political deals could be achieved more easily and appropriately by negotiations with the wives of powerful men. Unfortunately, these women usually ruined their husband's career and reputation by their greed and corruption.

Divorce is not common or acceptable in our society. It is considered shameful for the affected women, their families and relatives. Social and economic pressures on women created by a divorce are usually unbearable; they therefore make every effort to avoid it. If the broken marital tie cannot be mended, there is usually no divorce in the legal sense. The husband simply abandons his wife and marries another woman, or the wife just leaves and returns to her parents' home or goes else-where. She does not necessarily remarry. Children and related matters are usually settled between the two families without resort to courts. It is a well-established fact in our society that it is much more difficult for the divorced woman to remarry than for the divorced man. In the absence of her husband, she will take over all his responsibility and if she has grown-up sons, the oldest usually replaces the father[5] to take care of his young siblings, who owe him respect and obedience.

4. The Vietnamese Children

Generally speaking, Vietnamese children are polite and be-have themselves at home and outside of their home. They are subject to strict discipline, especially at school, and are taught to be absolutely obedient to their older siblings, relatives, and parents. Disobedience to parents is regarded as a serious viola-tion of the moral code. They are also told to obey, respect, and listen to older people. Interference or interruption by small children in conversation between older people is considered

[5] See p. 25.

to be impolite and accordingly censured. Most children are shy, especially young girls, in the presence of a stranger or when they meet someone for the first time. They are passive because they are afraid to offend older people, disturb the harmony, or make fools of themselves.

Even at an early age, children are taught to be loyal to their families and assume responsibility toward themselves, their relatives, parents, and others.

At home children are expected to help their parents, take care of their younger siblings or aging grandparents, and do whatever they can in the way of babysitting, cooking, cleaning, washing, and so on and so forth, depending on their age and the economic situation of their families. This is true especially in low or lower income families where domestic help is not readily available. For instance, it is not uncommon for a young girl of four or five to be assigned to take care of her sibling one or two years younger than she. As a rule, girls tend to have to do more household work than boys so that the latter can have more time for their studies or other activities. Again, here is another example of the old conception that girls do not need a good education and that boys' studies are considered more important than those of girls. Older girls are expected to acquaint themselves with housework, cooking, and needlework, even if domestic help is available, so that they can prepare themselves for "serving their future husbands and in-laws." Boys, on the other hand, are not allowed to enter the kitchen. If they choose to do so, they will immediately be asked to leave, because this is one of the off-limit areas for boys.

In regard to all important decisions concerning their children, Vietnamese parents are supposed to have absolute authority. However, they usually consult their children before making any decisions. If there is disagreement between parents and their children, the former will resort to persuasive power or call upon filial piety, or even exercise their authority to make their point, or they will just simply compromise with their children, depending on the individual case or how obedient the children are to their parents.

It is the traditional duty and responsibility of the parents not only toward their sons but also toward their ancestors, to select proper and good wives for their sons to carry on the family line and traditions. As a rule, the choice is primarily focused on the virtues of their would-be daughters-in-law. Physical appearance plays only a secondary role in this decision. Parents therefore traditionally arrange marriages for their children either by themselves or with the help of a matchmaker or "go-between." Usually, this person is a female and must exercise great caution in doing her important job because if the pre-arranged marriage does not work out, she has to take all the blame. If it does work out, the married couple owe her respect and gratitude. We have a much-repeated saying that "children sit where their parents place them." Even nowadays, pre-arranged marriages between families are still a common practice. However, there has been some relaxation of the parents' absolute authority. Vietnamese parents now tend to give their children (under strict supervision) opportunities to get to know their would-be spouses before any final decision is made. As recently as twenty years ago, children usually had no opportunity to meet their future spouses before marriage. They just "sat where their parents placed them."

When the parents get old and cannot work, the children proudly take good care of their parents. Nursing homes are practically nonexistent in Vietnam. Abandoning elderly parents is considered shameful and a social disgrace.

At school, children show great respect for their teachers and school administrators. Discipline is strictly observed, and any violations will result in severe punishments. Criticism by children of the teachers or school administrators, whether justifiable or unjustifiable, is not desirable or even acceptable.

Courting and dating are never encouraged by the parents nor practiced by the majority of young people. In fact, American-style dating does not exist among high school students and might be found only among a handful of college students. Casual friendship between boys and girls does exist but usually on a reserved basis and under strict control by parents or surveillance by school proctors. Girls tend to get together with girls, boys tend to flock with boys, and the dividing line in most cases is clear-cut. Any attempt to cross this line with public knowledge might lead to damaging jokes or make the young person a laughing-stock. Alcoholic consumption, congregating in bars, attending social dances or parties for young people are either unknown or not common. Western-style dancing is practiced only by a very limited number of youngsters, particularly of high social class, and until recent times has generally been considered corruptive.

The American terms "boy friend" and "girl friend" cannot be found in the Vietnamese lexicon. Outings by mixed groups are permissible and not unusual. By and large, even though college students enjoy much more freedom than high school students, they are still inclined to observe the social conventions and moral codes. Shaking hands even with members of the same sex is not widely practiced. Boys do not shake hands with the opposite sex and vice versa. Girls do not shake hands at all. Physical contacts and touching are usually avoided, especially between male teachers and girl students of about twelve years of age or older. However, one can often see two young friends of the same sex, male as well as female, hold each other's hands while walking in the street. This is a gesture of close friendship and there is absolutely nothing wrong with it.

III

Vietnamese Characteristics

Under this broad classification, we will deal with different aspects of behavioral patterns and social conventions of the Vietnamese people as well as their forms of address and language. To many Americans, some of these characteristics may be quite bewildering and hard to understand. In their daily contacts with Vietnamese friends, they may not find exactly what is described below. If that is so, it is probably because their Vietnamese friends behave in a manner slightly different from their traditional way in Vietnam in order to adjust to their newly acquired environment and condition. Generally speaking, their basic and traditional characteristics will remain with them for a long time, even indefinitely if efforts are made to maintain their tradition and unique culture.

1. Personal Traits

Basically speaking the Vietnamese are a very polite and sensitive people. In any social contact, they prize good manners above all, and judge you to a large extent by your courtesy. Politeness is considered a must for good social conduct. The Vietnamese do not look straight into the eyes of the person with whom they conduct a conversation; doing so is considered very impolite and might cause uneasiness on the other's part if he is Vietnamese. In the United States, however, such behavior is completely acceptable and regarded as a sign of straightforwardness. Since the Vietnamese are a sensitive and gentle people, criticism and humiliation, especially in public, are regarded as extremely impolite and could lead to embarrassment or anger. Therefore, if criticism need be offered, it should be given in private. The Vietnamese can be embarrassed easily, especially young females.

It is widely known that Vietnamese do not generally make their feelings known to others, especially to those with whom they do not already have a close relationship. They avoid displaying feelings in public, whether it be anger, dissatisfaction, jubilation, or affection. They are reticent about imposing or causing offense. They believe that to do so will cause disharmony between themselves and the people they deal with. Depending on their relationship with you, the Vietnamese might reluctantly do something which deep in their hearts they would prefer to avoid. They do it because they are afraid of displeasing you or because they want to avoid confrontation. They rarely show their reluctance. However, they care for other people's feelings and will make every effort not to hurt or embarrass anyone. Sparing someone's feelings is usually valued more than factual truth, a fact which often creates misunderstanding and occasional bitterness. If necessary they will even resort to honoring lies or to making up stories just for the sake of protecting others' feelings. Nevertheless, they are not only easygoing but easy to get along with.

When a Vietnamese person's feelings have been hurt, he will remember it for a long time. It is usually difficult to restore a broken relationship or a lost confidence.

Modesty and humility are emphasized in the culture of the Vietnamese and deeply ingrained into their natural behavior. Therefore, bragging is often criticized and avoided. When being praised for something, a Vietnamese often declines to accept praise by humbly claiming that he does not warrant such esteem. The Vietnamese do not customarily demonstrate their knowledge, skills, or possessions without being asked to do so.

The Vietnamese in general are characterized by their cheerfulness, romantic character, ability to stand hardship, self-content, resourcefulness, adaptability, and flexibility. This romantic character is often reflected in the melody of their music and in literature. Although there have been some complaints of stubbornness by some Westerners who have come into contact or who work with the Vietnamese, they are, by and large, thought of as a considerate, gentle, and responsive people.

In the Vietnamese approach to life, reason does not necessarily outweigh sentiment and emotion. On the contrary, quite often sentiment or emotion is given priority consideration.

Under the influence of Buddhist teachings, the Vietnamese believe that whatever happens to them in this life is the direct result of their actions in their last life. In addition to this, each person is fully responsible for his own destiny and action in this life, which in turn will determine his fate in the next. This is his guidance in the present life. It is probably because of this belief that he does not seem to have a strong sense of responsibility for people who are not related to him either by blood or marriage.

The Vietnamese take things as they come and seem to Americans not to take things seriously. If things go wrong even after many efforts have been made, they attribute it to fate. This attitude may suggest the reason why foreigners who have come into contact with the Vietnamese tend to think them a passive people.

The many long wars, the foreign dominations, and extensive propaganda in the history of their country have made the Vietnamese distrust people from other lands and even their own countrymen if they do not know these people well enough. Consequently, they usually do not feel at ease and talk very little in the presence of a stranger. They will hide their guarded reservation by shyness or politeness. Even so, they are well known for their hospitality, which can be warmly accorded even to the newly acquainted or to foreigners.

The Vietnamese tend to think that Westerners are naive or without "depth." This is probably because of the West's dynamic and materialistic approach and the Western tendency often to judge people at face value. The Vietnamese are basically very capable, industrious, and eager to learn. If properly motivated, they can be valuable assets to their employers. They are traditionally loyal to their employers and devoted to their jobs. This type of loyalty and devotion leads them to sacrifice if necessary. For instance, they will voluntarily stay on their jobs without being asked to work extra hours to finish work which needs to be done.

Manual jobs are looked down upon and usually reserved for the less educated or people of low social class, while white collar jobs are considered "decent." Of those Vietnamese who have sought refuge in the United States, a good number are in the less educated or illiterate group. These people need special attention in the adjustment process.

Vietnamese do not change jobs very often and tend to be reluctant to do so. For them their jobs are their lives and they stick to them. In Vietnam, employers played a paternalistic role, taking care of the welfare of their employees and sometimes that of their families as well. It was not unusual for an employer to arrange and take care of marriages for his employees or even preside over the marriage ceremonies. If an employee became sick or disabled, the employer continued to provide financial assistance. The Vietnamese are very dexterous and patient. They are a hard-working people, but if there is not sufficient motivation and an appropriate boost, they could be considered lazy by others.

The Vietnamese like fun and know how to enjoy life in their own way. Vietnamese cuisine, although having its own particular characteristics, is influenced by two of the best kinds of cooking in the world, namely Chinese and French. It is considered to be one of the best cuisines in the world by such food authorities as Craig Claiborne of *The New York Times.*

Competition is not a Vietnamese tradition and is not considered a driving force for progress. "Keeping up with the Joneses" is usually ridiculed among Vietnamese. They are generous in helping individuals but generally do not volunteer their services like the Americans. The rich and even the very rich did not give away large sums of money to organizations or charity agencies. Organizations like this were very few and were generally supported by the government. As a matter of fact, needy individuals in Vietnam are usually taken care of by their families or friends. This may partly explain why charity organizations are not needed as in the U.S.A. Public assistance has been virtually unknown in Vietnam. Only recently, because of frequent uprootings due to devastating wars and political upheavals, have some Vietnamese needed this type of assistance but only to a very limited extent. Generally, they are reluctant to receive such aid and accept it only in case of desperation.

The Vietnamese tend to be quiet, law-abiding and nonviolent. Violence is not their way of life. They do not like to watch violent scenes nor do they like litigation. They only resort to it when all other means have been exhausted outside the court. Litigation has often been discouraged and ridiculed in literature.

2. Customs

The Vietnamese usually speak in a low voice. Talkative women are usually discredited and criticized. A raised voice is generally considered undesirable and impolite. Speaking with excessive gestures, especially in the case of women, is not a Vietnamese mode of expression and is considered Westernized, if not bad manners. It should be noted that in Vietnam, beckoning with a finger or waving somebody to you with your palm upward could be interpreted as an insult, since such gestures are used primarily to call dogs or other animals. For a Vietnamese to be placed on the same level with animals is a serious offense. Waving with the palm down, however, is quite acceptable.

Only a few urban people, influenced by Western customs, celebrate birthdays, since that occasion is not a Vietnamese custom. Nor do Vietnamese send Christmas cards.[1] Wedding and funeral ceremonies are important events and are usually performed with solemn and traditional rituals.

The Vietnamese celebrate Tết, the lunar calendar New Year (which may fall in January or February). For every Vietnamese, regardless of his religion or social class, Tết is the most important holiday festival, which lasts for a minimum of three days. During this period, all stores are closed and

---

[1] Nevertheless, in Vietnam, even though the large majority are not Christians, Christmas is an official major holiday.

business interrupted. Tết is not a religious holiday but is colored by all sorts of religious and superstitious practices. Catholic masses are conducted in churches on New Year's Eve and New Year's Day. Buddhists and Confucianists likewise go to temples in great numbers to pray for health, prosperity, longevity, and happiness. At home, the head of the family, male or female, traditionally sets up a family altar with food and fruit in the open air. At midnight of New Year's Eve, when firecrackers begin to explode continuously and noisily, he or she starts to perform religious rituals in front of the altar to worship Buddha, various known and unknown gods and ancestors, and to pray for the new year. Children are allowed to stay up past midnight and anxiously wait for the traditional money gifts, given out by their parents or elders only after midnight. Similar to the Christian tradition of Christmas gifts for children, the amount of gift money each child receives supposedly measures his conduct and performance during the past year. Children and youngsters are told to behave themselves and be very careful in what they do or say on New Year's Day since their conduct will be reflected throughout the year and bring good or bad luck. In other words, the Vietnamese believe that whatever happens or is said on this first day of the year will repeat itself and influence their lives throughout the new year. Bad things should be strictly avoided.

Customarily, people of higher rank in the family give money gifts to those of lower rank, not necessarily vice versa. They wish each other all sorts of good things appropriate for the individual case. The first person who comes and visits the family on New Year's Day will bring them good or bad luck for the year depending on his moral conduct and wealth. Since they strongly believe in this, the Vietnamese usually select very carefully and in advance the person, very often a man, who they know is a good person and successful in life. They ask him to come and "open the door of their home." When this person comes, he exchanges wishes with the family and is frequently offered some food or drink to toast the new year. If during the year, this family is stricken by misfortune, the visitor might have to take all the blame and will not be invited next year. Because of this belief, many people are reluctant to respond to requests to act as the first visitors of the year.

Children of the family usually expect money gifts from visitors to their home during the first three days of the year. This is the most appropriate occasion for friends to visit friends, for relatives to get together with relatives, for business people to treat each other generously, and for practically everything. People will visit the most important persons for them on the first day, the second most important ones on the following day, and then for the third day, etc. These Tết visits are taken very seriously. If, for one reason or another, you cannot come to offer your wishes to someone you are supposed to visit, this person's feelings may be hurt. In the United States it is quite acceptable to send a card on the Tết occasion.

Pre-Tết is the time for decorating the house, polishing altar brassware, and cleaning up; it is the time for paying off all debts and returning all borrowed things, since it is believed that by not doing so, there will be more debts next year. It is the time to evaluate achievements, failures, and mistakes of the passing year, to forgive others for their mischief or offense and to re-establish peace or reconcile with adversaries. It is also the time for a shopping spree. The Vietnamese, whether needy or well-to-do, tend to spend extravagant amounts of money on new clothes, food, and presents. Such presents, usually in the form of food, poultry, or fruit, are customarily delivered to the recipient about a week or ten days before Tết. It is the time for enjoyment and forgetting about all worries or miseries, and for putting on one's best and newest clothes and showing one's wealth by spending lavishly. It is the time for children and adults to indulge in gambling and to play favorite games of cards for money. It is also time for enjoying traditional food especially prepared for Tết. The preparation of food might require days before Tết and its consumption lasts throughout the holiday. It is a very colorful festive time indeed!

Vietnam has a number of secular and religious holidays but none can be compared to Tết.

The Vietnamese, basically speaking, are a casual, friendly, and hospitable people. For them friendship is very important. They form very strong friendships and take pride in their hospitality. If they consider you to be their friend, you can share things with them. For them, friendship is not only necessary for their emotional needs but also for future assistance. There is a saying in Vietnamese that "far away relatives are not as important as nearby neighbors." This saying is particularly meaningful in the light of the importance of the family in Vietnamese culture. When they are invited to a friend's or relative's home for a meal, celebration, or commemorative occasion, they take some gifts, usually food or fruit, for the host's family. Their homes are always open to friends. Visitors whether announced or unexpected are usually received warmly. No appointments are necessary for casual visits to their homes, and if you happen to be there at meal time, you will be graciously invited to sit down and share whatever is available on the table. When they offer you something, particularly food, they sincerely want you to enjoy it. They will be very pleased to see that you enjoy what is offered to you.

Indeed, they will not feel at ease if they notice you do not really care for it. In case there is not enough food, they will not hesitate to offer you their own portions to make sure that you have enough to eat. For them all this is a sincere manifestation of hospitality and close friendship. This behavior derives from a sincere intention of pleasing you.

On top of this, when giving gifts, they will usually disparage the gift, pretending it is of no great value, even though its value may obviously be very costly and lavish. For instance, if they give you something valuable that you did not expect, they will say something like, "Oh, this is a very small gift of no great monetary value." They are taught to be grateful and appreciate what is done for them or given to them. Sometimes this gratitude lasts a lifetime. They hope to have a chance to pay back "their debts." Many Vietnamese are reluctant to accept help from individuals because of this fear of gratitude.

Self-respect has traditionally been accorded a high standing in the Vietnamese system of virtues. The Vietnamese are not generous with praise. Praising someone profusely or in his presence is regarded as flattery and sometimes even mockery. If a Vietnamese is praised for his achievements or for any other reasons, he usually shows his modesty by declining the praise or claiming that he does not deserve it. Westerners sometimes have difficulty understanding this. It is considered insincere, or bad form, to praise highly or to appear to be overly grateful. Furthermore, Vietnamese do not say "thank you" for everything. Saying so all the time is considered to be flowery and an indication of a lack of sincerity. For instance, if you do something for someone and he says "thank you," you do not say "thank you" to him in return.

Many things that are fairly common in American cities are

sure to be shocking to the average Vietnamese. Heavy drinking and public intoxication are good examples. The Vietnamese are not heavy drinkers. Drunkenness or alcoholism is a social disgrace and a dishonor for the affected people and their families. The majority of Vietnamese women never sip alcohol and usually shy away when alcoholic beverages are offered to them. Drinking women are despised in our society. Drinking problems are rare and practically nonexistent among women and confined to only a handful of men.

While smoking has gained wide acceptance among men, very few Vietnamese women smoke; those who do are generally older women. Women's smoking in public has been traditionally considered something "unusual."

The Vietnamese do not keep pets like Americans and are not very fond of domesticated animals. They will never understand how their American friends can spend so much time and money taking care of their pets, let alone how they can develop an emotional attachment to these animals.

Homosexuality and bisexuality, unheard of in Vietnamese society, are definitely considered "shocking" and could never be accepted by the Vietnamese.

Going out to dine or to a bar are not common practices because the Vietnamese are basically home-oriented. As a matter of fact, Western-style bars were only imported to Vietnam very recently to serve foreigners. In Vietnam, "good" women do not go to bars. They might go to a discotheque or tearoom to enjoy a musical show or dance, but they are usually accompanied by friends or relatives. This practice, in any case, is restricted to a few big cities. In small towns or rural areas, bars, discotheques, or even tearooms do not exist. Western-style dances are not widespread and are only enjoyed by a limited number of Vietnamese in cosmopolitan areas. For traditional Vietnamese, this type of dance might even be considered "corruptive."

"Dutch treat" is definitely not a Vietnamese custom and might lead to embarrassment. In Vietnam, when you invite someone to go out to a movie or restaurant, you are expected to pay the bill unless sharing the cost is made clear at the moment of the invitation. Even so, this practice is not common. Your Vietnamese friend will be surprised and confused if you ask him to go out with you and then you let him split the bill. As a rule, if you pay this time, he will pay next time. He is not accustomed to paying his own share when taking a taxi together with friends or others. If he invites you out and offers to pay, let him do so even if it is obviously hard on him; otherwise he might feel uneasy about his hospitality or feel that perhaps you think he cannot afford it.

Vietnamese customs and habits are likely to be shocking in some ways to Americans. The average Vietnamese has a conception of time that is very different from the average American's, and thus he is unlikely to be on time for all of his appointments. The Vietnamese are noted for their "rubber watch"; that is to say, an appointment time can be flexible or stretch from half an hour to more than one hour. Punctuality is neither often honored nor necessarily required. The Vietnamese are not as time-conscious as Americans, having a take-it-easy approach to life. They will seldom be on time for social or business appointments. The exception is an appointment deemed important to them. In Vietnam, if you invite someone for dinner, say at 7:30 P.M., do not expect him or her to be there much earlier than 8:00 P.M. since he is probably afraid that his arrival on time might be misinterpreted as being too enthusiastic, something to be avoided.

Do not be shocked, angry, or even surprised if a Vietnamese "forgets" to get back to you with an answer that he has repeatedly been asked to give, especially when a negative answer is involved. He would rather not communicate with you than take the chance of having a confrontation.

If you want to offer a Vietnamese something, he may refuse it the first time or even the second time, claiming he does not need it or deserve it, although in fact he may be happy to accept your offer. You will likely be successful if you have the patience to repeat the offer once more. If this time he insistently declines it, then he really means it. He tends to think that if he accepts your offer the first time (especially when he is offered some food), he might be regarded as "greedy." This is a part of their natural way of life and quite acceptable.

3. Physical Contact

There is an old saying that males should be separated from females and vice versa, and physical contact between opposite sexes avoided. Actual practice goes even further than that. Physical contact between grown-up relatives or friends, or between the same or opposite sexes, is thus not a common sight.

While men, particularly the educated and urban, have become accustomed to the Western practice of handshaking, women normally do not shake hands, especially with one another. A few "sophisticated and civilized" women might extend their hands first to men, but the latter should be careful about taking the initiative; otherwise they might find that their friendly gesture does not meet with a response. Even where handshaking is a common practice, a man of lower status (in terms of age, position, wealth) does not normally offer his hand first since this initiative is deemed impolite or inappropriate. Older men usually do not shake hands but will greet each other by joining hands in front of them and bowing slightly. The same greeting gesture can also be observed between two men or a woman and a man. Younger people usually smile and incline slightly to greet one another. The Vietnamese greet the head of the family or an older person first, then people of lower rank. All this is accompanied by the use of the appropriate forms of greeting.[2]

The Vietnamese do not put their arms around the shoulders of the adults who are not their relatives or close friends. Slapping someone on the shoulder or on the back if done by a man of higher status or by a friend might be permissible as a paternalistic gesture or manifestation of close friendship, but it will definitely cause offense if a man of lower status does so to his superiors. Touching small children even on the head is quite acceptable but should be avoided with older children.[3] Hugging or kisses on the cheek in greeting are unknown in the culture of the Vietnamese. Kissing or embracing between the two sexes in public is considered an offense.

Although physical contact or touching between the same or different sexes in public is generally regarded as a taboo and frowned upon, it is not uncommon to see two young friends of the same sex, either male or female, holding hands in the street in Vietnam. For the Vietnamese this behavior is quite natural and has nothing to do with homosexuality or lesbianism.[4] On the contrary, it is a gesture of close friendship. However, this practice is generally confined to unmarried youngsters.

[2] See "Forms of Address," pp. 49-55.
[3] See also pp. 31-32.
[4] *Ibid.*

Young unmarried people of the opposite sex do not normally hold hands and never touch each other in public.

4. Vietnamese Smile, Laugh, and Giggle

The Vietnamese are smiling people and well known for their perpetual and all-purpose smile, a useful tool for them and a puzzle to outsiders. The smile can be used to express or cover up feelings, emotions, truth, ignorance, repentance, confusion, disappointment, pride, fear, wrongdoing, just about anything—or it may mean nothing.

This puzzling smile often can be seen in all circumstances that one can possibly imagine: pleasant or unpleasant, happy or unhappy, serious or unimportant, delightful or bitter. In other words, the Vietnamese smile very often and about practically anything.

While it is hard for non-Vietnamese to detect the real meaning of a smile, a Vietnamese usually has a feeling about what the smile of his fellow countryman implies. Either the circumstance or cause for such a smile or its strangeness can serve as a hint for a Vietnamese but at the same time be quite misleading for a non-Vietnamese. A Vietnamese smiles when he greets somebody he knows or meets for the first time. His smile is an expression of friendliness or serves to make others feel comfortable. He will smile when a foreigner does not do something correctly or properly, for instance, if he mispronounces a name or handles chopsticks clumsily. He will resort to smiling to show his interest or disinterest in something. He smiles when he wants to encourage someone to do something or when he is displeased. He smiles just to please others or not to hurt them. The Vietnamese smile even when they see someone falling in the street because this person looks funny when he falls, not because of any ill wishes. The smile will appear on his face when he does not wish to say "No," a word usually regarded as unpleasant in Vietnamese culture. Therefore he often agrees, even though in fact he does not wish to do so. If he expresses his agreement by saying "yes" with a smile, for instance, it might be that he does not want to offend you. Whether or not he will carry out his agreement is another story. It depends on how much he respects you or what he owes you in terms of job, gratitude, friendship. His smile can very well serve as a polite tool to refuse to answer a certain question, to avoid doing something, to mask scorn for someone or something, to hide his bitterness, and so on.

Similarly, the Vietnamese like to laugh and they laugh easily. However, they do not laugh as often as they smile. Their laughter is usually not noisy or loud, but often well controlled because noisy laughter can be considered bothersome or impolite. Women do not normally laugh as frequently, or as easily, as men because in the Vietnamese culture women are traditionally expected to be gentle and quiet. In situations where men laugh, Vietnamese women smile instead. Like the smile, laughter can serve as a wonderful means to express or hide emotions or feelings. But it generally occurs more often on the occasion of a pleasant experience or to express feelings: excitement, enjoyment, fun, pleasure, tickling, rather than for purposes of covering-up. A person who can laugh about his own sufferings, misfortunes, failures, and mistakes is admired by the Vietnamese.

Finally, giggling is normally confined to females, especially young girls. It serves more or less the same purposes as those of the smile or laughter. It is generally a sign of shyness.

On top of this, the Vietnamese are fond of humor; they are equipped with a light-hearted sense of humor. And, of course, a happening or a story which can offer a tremendous source of amusement for a Vietnamese may very well seem humorless or even be considered "bad taste" in other cultures.

Non-Vietnamese may experience frustration or even irritation when they try to understand the exact meaning of an enigmatic smile, laughter, or giggle at a humorous joke at times or in circumstances which, for them, do not seem at all appropriate. This is an integral part of the Vietnamese culture which reflects itself unmistakably in two popular philosophical sayings: "Half-closed and half-open offers more excitement," and "The naked truth hurts."

5. *Forms of Address*

Traditionally, the Vietnamese have been concerned more with status than wealth. Strict observance of, and conformity to rituals and etiquette are their way of life. Social and family hierarchies have been the main force for maintaining family harmony and social order.[5] These hierarchies have always been spelled out clearly, leaving no chance for misunderstandings or arguments. The family hierarchy is based on one's relationship to other members of the family in terms of sex, age, generation, paternal or maternal side, and marriage. The Vietnamese language is equipped with a complex system of kinship terms reflecting clearly one's relation to others in the family. For example:

Tôi: I (Semantically, it means "servant")
Anh: older brother
Chị: older sister

[5] See pp. 9-10.

Em: younger siblings
   Em trai: younger brother
   Em gái: younger sister
Bác: older sibling of mother or father
Cậu: younger brother of mother,[6] etc.

The social hierarchy uses an equally complex system of forms of address and titles based on sex, status, age, and occupation of the person being addressed as well as one's relationship to him or her.[7]

The following are the three commonly used formal forms of address:

Ông: Mr. to—
   young or middle-aged man
   man of higher social position
   casual male acquaintance or male business acquaint-
      ance of long standing

Bā: Mrs. to—
   wife of *Ông*
   middle-aged woman obviously older than oneself
   married woman of casual acquaintance or sometimes
      a female business acquaintance of long standing

Cô: Miss to—
   young unmarried woman usually a few years younger
      than the speaker.[8]

---

[6] See *Vietnamese in a Nutshell* by Vuong Gia Thuy, Institute For Language Study, Montclair, N.J., 1975, pp. 45-48.

[7] *Ibid.*, pp. 47-49.

[8] *Ibid.*, p. 47.

It is interesting to note that these three social forms of address (*Ông* "Mr.," *Bā* "Mrs." and *Cô* "Miss") are also the terms to indicate blood relationship:

Ông: grandfather
Bā: grandmother
Cô: aunt

People are reluctant to call their new acquaintances by name without the appropriate forms of address listed above.

In the Vietnamese way, the family name is written first, followed by a middle name (sometimes omitted), then a given name. Thus:

Vương Gia *Thụy* (Family/Middle/*Given*)[9]

compared to:

Michael M. *Jones* (Given/Middle/*Family*)

The family name is never used except in a few rare instances, as in *Uncle Hồ* (Hồ is a family name of *Hồ* Chí Minh). The most popular Vietnamese family names are Nguyễn, Lê, Lý, Trần, Ngô, Đinh, Trịnh, Phạm, Vũ, among others. It is interesting to note that the family name *Nguyễn* is the most popular of all. It is even more popular than *Brown, Jones,* or *Smith.* Historically, whenever there was a change of dynasty, people

---

[9] When you come across a Vietnamese name in the U.S.A., be alert because the chances are that the Vietnamese order might have been switched to conform with the American way: *Thuy Gia Vuong* (American way) instead of *Vuong Gia Thuy* (Vietnamese way). If there is any doubt, ask the person concerned.

who were the members of the families of the old rulers or were closely associated with them had to change their family names to avoid reprisals or persecutions. They usually picked new names or even adopted the family names of the new dynasties as a show of loyalty to the new rulers. In fact, the Nguyen dynasty was the last and one of the longest dynasties in Vietnam.

If the middle name is *Văn* (meaning literature),[10] it is a male name, while the middle name *Thị* (meaning female) indicates without doubt that the person who carries this name is a female.

Vietnamese given names usually have a meaning, for instance, *Hồng* "rose," *Hùng* "Hero," *Tiến* "progress," etc. Except for a limited number of given names which indicate clearly the sex of the people who carry these names, for instance, *Hùng, Thông* or *Chí* for males, and *Nương, Hằng* or *Hương* for females, the same names can usually be used for both males and females, for example *Lộc, Thu, Phúc, Dung,* etc.

In formal situations, the given name of the person addressed or his full name preceded by a formal form of address (*Ông* "Mr.," *Bā* "Mrs." or *Cô* "Miss") is used: *Ông Thụy* "Mr. *Thụy*" (equivalent to Mr. *Michael*) or Mr. *Vương Gia Thụy*. In informal or friendly situations (when the speaker and the person addressed are on more or less the same level) forms of

---

[10] In the old days, generally speaking, only males were given the chance to be educated, and since education in Vietnam was mainly of a literary nature, the middle name *Văn* has traditionally been given to male babies with the implication that they would later pursue a literary career or become white collar workers instead of engaging in manual jobs, traditionally looked down upon in Vietnamese society.

address or titles are not used, and the given name alone is permissible:

Thụy, hộ tôi cái nāy: "Thuy, please help me with this."

Frequently, the forms of addressing relatives are also used to address acquaintances or nonrelatives in order to show respect or friendliness to these people. For example:

Bác Thụy: Uncle Thuy
Em Hoa: Younger sibling Hoa
Chị Ba: Older sister Ba

If the person addressed has an honorary, elective, or professional title such as *Chủ Tịch* "chairman," *Bác Sĩ* "medical doctor," *Tiến Sĩ* "Ph.D. holder," *Thầy* "teacher," etc., the title is used before the name:

Bác sĩ Cường: Dr. Cuong (*Cuong* is the given name
of an M.D. whose full name is *Tran Trong Cuong*).
Thầy Hiền: Teacher Hien (*Hien* is the given name of
a high school teacher whose full name is *Dao Van
Hien*).

Sometimes the forms of address are placed just before the title to be more specific about, or to indicate the sex of, the person addressed:

Ông Bác sĩ Cường: Dr. Cuong (the male)
Bā Giáo sủ Huy: Professor Huy (the female) or (the
wife of Professor Huy)

The polite term *Thửa* (similar to "Please") preceding all forms of address or titles adds more politeness to the context and is frequently used to address people of higher status or superiors. In this case the given name is usually omitted.

> *Thửa* Bác sĩ: Please Doctor or Doctor
> *Thửa* Giáo sư: Please Professor or Professor

Similarly, in giving orders or asking somebody to do something, do not use his given name but simply the appropriate forms of address (Mr., Mrs., Miss) or titles (Doctor, President, Professor).

> *Ông* hộ tôi cái nãy: "Sir, please help me with this."
> (Mr.)
> *Bác sĩ* đậu xe chỗ nãy: "Doctor, park your car here."

In addition, one should avoid calling older people by name or first name alone because this is considered impolite. The appropriate form of address or title must be used instead, with or without the given name. A word of caution is in order here: the use of the appropriate terms of address or titles is of utmost importance in any social contacts since its misuse could create embarrassment and irritation on the part of the person being addressed.

A general greeting term, *Chāo* (pronounced *Chow*), always precedes all forms of address and titles and can be used for all cases. It is equivalent to "Hello" or "Hi" in English but on a more formal basis. *Chāo* can be used at any point of time of the day to greet people or take leave. The Vietnamese language does not have separate greeting terms applicable to different parts of the days (morning, afternoon, evening, and night) as in English. For example:

Chào Ông: Hello, Sir or Good-bye, Sir
Chào Bác sĩ: Hello, Doctor or Good-bye, Doctor

If one wishes to show respect to someone, the term *Kính* "respectfully," will be used immediately before the complete phrase of greeting:

Kính chào Ông: Hello, Sir
Kính chào Bác sĩ: Hello, Doctor

6. Language

A number of languages are spoken in Vietnam, but the official and most predominant one is Vietnamese, the language spoken by a large majority of the 40 million people. Tribesmen living in remote areas have their own languages, which are spoken by a very limited number of people. There has been a widespread misconception in the United States that French is spoken by a large number of Vietnamese. This is not true. By and large, the elite or educated of older generations know French well but usually do not use this foreign language in their communications with each other. The younger generation tends to be more interested in English than in French, both taught at schools, even though only a few know English well.

Chinese is the mother tongue of the Chinese minority, who are also usually fluent in Vietnamese. Other foreign languages which are taught in Vietnam but only to a very limited extent are German, Spanish, and Japanese.[11]

Contrary to the general misconception, the Vietnamese lan-

---

[11] This statement applies to South Vietnam before the fall of the Saigon regime in May, 1075. Details of the new educational system in the whole of Vietnam are not yet available.

guage does not sound like Cantonese nor is it related to the Chinese language. Vietnamese is a language whose origin, even today, is not clearly or satisfactorily established. It has appropriated many words from the Chinese (mainly Cantonese) in much the same way that English borrowed from French. As with other languages, when the Vietnamese borrow words of foreign origin, the tendency is to change its original pronunciation to fit the Vietnamese sound system.

Vietnamese has three main dialects peculiar to three different geographical areas: the North, Center, and South. Although dialects can differ in some forms, either in pronunciation or vocabulary, there is probably no greater difference between them than there is, say, between American and British English. In other words, throughout Vietnam, the members of one dialect group can communicate with another group without any difficulty.[12]

It was only recently, about half a century ago, that Vietnam began widely to use a modified Roman alphabet as its writing system. Before that it had used Chinese characters or modified Chinese characters. The modified Roman alphabet has been overwhelmingly accepted and is quite well established. As a consequence, it has become the sole writing of the Vietnamese.

Generally speaking, the Vietnamese alphabet is more phonetic than that of English. This means that in Vietnamese each alphabetical letter or combination of two letters such as *ph* (pronounced as *f*) represents only one sound, while an English letter can have more than one. For instance, the letter *a* is pronounced more or less the same way in Vietnamese while it can have different sounds in English:

[12] See *Vietnamese in a Nutshell*, Vuong G. Thuy, Institute for Language Study, Montclair, N.J., 1975, pp. 11-29 and pp. 124-133.

Vietnamese: *a* (ah); *ao* (pond); *am* (nunnery) have all
same pronunciation for *a*
English: *a*t; f*a*r; g*a*te have different sounds for *a*

Clusters of consonants are very rare, and only a limited
number of consonants can exist in final positions. They are
ng/ŋ/ as in ki*ng*, -*nh/ñ/* (similar to -ny- in ca*ny*on), ch/č/
as in chur*ch*, *c/k/*, *m*, *n*, *p* and *t*. Therefore, the final consonants, clusters of consonants, and inconsistency of phonetic
representation in English spelling will likely create serious
problems for the Vietnamese learner.[13]
Vietnamese is basically a monosyllabic language, that is to
say, there is one syllable per word. For example: *đi* "go,"
hát "sing," *e* "be afraid that," *tách* "separate from." For the
American perhaps the most interesting aspect of the Vietnamese language is its tones. Vietnamese is a tone language.
That is, each word is formed with at least one vowel followed
by a musical pitch or tone which is meaningful and forms part
of the word.[14] The number of Vietnamese tones varies from
one dialect to another and from four to six. Each tone is repre-
sented in the writing system by a diacritical mark over or under
one of the vowels of the word, or by the absence of this mark.
The following is a typical example of the Vietnamese tonal
system:

[13] Any sound or combination of sounds or linguistic feature in English
which does not exist in Vietnamese will, as a rule, cause difficulty for
the Vietnamese learner. For a better understanding of these problems,
see *Vietnamese in a Nutshell*, pp. 13-16, and *Teaching English Pronunciation to Vietnamese*, #4, Arlington, Virginia: Center for Applied Linguistics.
[14] *Vietnamese in a Nutshell*, pp. 18-20 and pp. 124-127.

ma: ghost (no tone)

má: cheek (high-rising tone)

mā: then, but (low-falling tone)

mả: tomb (mid-low tone)

mã: horse (Sino-Vietnamese) (high-rising tone followed by a glottal stop)

mạ: young rice plant (glottal stop)

If the tone of a certain word is not produced correctly, it might result in the pronunciation of a completely different word or a nonexisting word. Thus when a foreigner tries to speak or read Vietnamese, he or she should be very careful with the tones; otherwise a mispronunciation of the tones can cause a Vietnamese to blush.

Although this chapter is definitely not intended to go into a detailed study of all features of Vietnamese, a rather peculiar aspect of Vietnamese culture clearly reflecting on the linguistic behavior of its people should be noted here: when asked a negative tag question such as "It is not too late, is it?", a Vietnamese will typically give a negative answer (if that is what he wishes), beginning with a Vietnamese introductory term equivalent to "Yes" in English to be followed by the negative statement "It is not too late." In other words, his answer will be "Yes, it is not too late." The "Yes" at this peculiar place simply implies that he agrees with the one who posed the question as far as the content of the question is concerned, namely "it is too late." The Vietnamese speaker will tend to translate this linguistic habit of his into his English practice and cause confusion on the part of the English listeners.

Finally, Vietnamese is equipped with a fairly complex vocabulary to reflect Vietnamese values. To illustrate this, let us take the verb for "consuming food" as an example. While English has the verb "to eat" for all cases, Vietnamese has at least two, one of which specifically expresses respect for age or status to the person(s) addressed:

Ông *ăn* cơm chưa? "Have you eaten yet?" (standard term) (you/eat/rice/yet)

Ông *xơi* cơm chưa? "Have you eaten yet?" (respectful term) (you/eat/rice/yet)

The respectful term *xơi* is never used with the first person, singular or plural, since the self is supposed to be humble. The sentences below would therefore sound odd to the Vietnamese ear even though they are grammatically correct.

Tôi *xơi* cơm rồi. "I have already eaten." (I/eat/rice/already)

Chúng tôi *xơi* cơm rồi. "We have already eaten." (We/eat/rice/already)

IV

Education

Educated people and scholars have traditionally been well respected and honored in Vietnamese society. Good education has always been considered most important and accordingly given the highest status in Vietnam.

1. In General

By and large, the Vietnamese educational system during the last half of the century[1] was modeled after the French system. As recently as 1945, when Vietnam became independent, two different and parallel educational systems existed concurrently and served only a limited number of privileged people. One was French and the other Vietnamese. It was a well-known fact that the French schools, where French was the medium of instruction, were attended not only by French students but also by the children of the Vietnamese elite.

[1] This chapter will deal mainly with educational data in regions controlled by the Saigon government and only up to May, 1975, when the massive evacuation of Vietnamese began. The author does not have access to materials concerning the present educational system under the new regime in Vietnam.

While the programs of study in the French schools duplicated those of France, the programs of study in the Vietnamese schools were written and administered by the Department of National Education; nevertheless the French influence was quite obvious.

After Vietnam gained its independence, the number of French schools run by French teachers and school administrators was gradually reduced, and Vietnamese schools correspondingly increased to fill the gap and meet the needs of the new nation. Education in Vietnam since then flourished at a very impressive pace, involving the large majority of the population. Illiteracy was attacked at its root. Tremendous efforts and great achievements were made in many areas of education such as teacher training, translation of foreign textbooks into Vietnamese, and development of curricula. The replacement of French by Vietnamese as the language of instruction at the university level was completed by mid-1950.

Vietnamese education was based on three fundamental principles: humanist, national, and open-minded. With these three underlying principles, it emphasized respect for the personality of the student, development of national spirit, and growth of the democratic and scientific spirit. The following excerpt from the English version of *Elementary Education Curriculum*, Department of National Education, Saigon, 1960, will clarify these basic principles.

A. Education in Vietnam must be a *humanist* education, respecting the sacred character of the human being, regarding man as an end in himself, and aiming at the full development of man.

B. Education in Vietnam must be a *national* education, respecting the traditional values, assuring the continuity of man with his natural environment (his family, profession, and country), aiming at safeguarding the nation, its prosperity, and the collective promotion of its people.

C. Education in Vietnam must be an *open* education, respecting the scientific mind as a factor of progress, attempting to develop the social and democratic spirit, and welcoming all the authentic cultural values of the world.

Although the above only deals with primary education, its principles and emphasis are similar to those of secondary education.[2]

Primary education, in principle, was compulsory for all children from age five through the five primary school grades. This was not necessarily strictly enforced because of wars and various reasons arising out of warfare, such as scattering of the population and lack of facilities and/or funds. While primary education was free, not all high school education was free. There were two types of high schools, private and public (totally supported and run by the government). Admission to public schools was determined by competitive entrance examinations given yearly by the individual public school. These schools charged neither fees nor tuition, and were generally recognized for their high scholastic standing. They had highly qualified teachers, good equipment, a high standard of instruction, and prestige. Entrance to private high schools, on the other hand, was relatively easy. Their fees and tuition were

[2] "A Proposal for the Comprehensive Secondary School Curriculum in Vietnam." Unpublished doctoral dissertation by Duong Thieu Tong, Teachers' College, Columbia University, 1968, p. 155.

generally high. They had lower instructional standards than that of public schools. Attempts were made to raise their standards and ease the shortage of teaching staff at private schools by allowing public school teachers to teach a limited number of hours per week at these schools. Like their counterparts at public schools, private school teachers had to meet certain requirements and standards (usually below those for public school teachers) set up by the Department of National Education and subject to regular inspections or checks by officials of this department.

In recent years the university student population grew so rapidly that the expansion of government-supported universities and colleges could not keep pace with the rapidly increased enrollment. As a consequence, private universities and colleges mushroomed all over the country to satisfy these ever-growing demands for higher education. Like private high schools, private higher education institutions were subject to control by the Department of National Education, but they enjoyed much more freedom in terms of programs of study than did private high schools.

Vietnamese education has often been criticized for its literary nature, orientation toward examinations, its learning style, lack of diversity in terms of programs of study, the rigidity of its teaching methodology, and for placing too much emphasis on academic orientation instead of the development of individual skills in students.

Furthermore, under French influence, the Vietnamese educational system was generally viewed as serving mainly the elite who could afford it in terms of economic and academic ability, while American education has been geared to serve the masses. One characteristic of the Vietnamese system was the dominant role of the teacher in the classroom with little participation on the part of the student. Another characteristic was the stress on memorization and repetition. These were just a few features of education in Vietnam.

2. Department of National Education

Unlike the United States, Vietnam had a uniform educational system for primary and secondary education throughout the country. This national educational system was under the strict control of the Department of National Education. The department was the sole authority and had overall powers in matters of education. It handled practically anything and everything concerning education: from curriculum to training and recruitment of teachers, from examinations to issuing of diplomas, from placements to disciplinary action, from the selection to the printing and translation of textbooks, etc. It gave directions and guidance to all schools, private and public, academic and vocational. It also had the responsibility for supervising and controlling the functions of all private schools except some French schools. Because of this concentration of powers, the Department of National Education, with its uniform educational policies, sometimes ignored or failed to take into account the educational needs and special conditions of some regions, especially those far from Saigon where the department had its headquarters.

3. Curriculum

Vietnam had a homogeneous educational system in contrast with the heterogeneous education of the U.S.A. There was a uniform curriculum for all primary or elementary schools and another for all high schools throughout the country, whether they were public or private. Vietnamese was the medium of instruction at all levels of education. Vietnamese children started elementary education at the age of five or six and spent five years in primary schools. Each school year was divided into two semesters. The children went to school six days a week, and instruction usually did not last more than four hours each school day.[3] The subjects taught were the Vietnamese language, moral education and civics, history, geography, mathematics, drawing, science, physical education, home economics, and child care.[4] The last two courses were reserved for girls only. There were also extracurricular activities for girls and for boys. Elementary education offered a kind of general knowledge and was geared to preparation for secondary or high school education. At the end of five years, the child received an elementary school certificate.

At the age of ten or eleven, the child entered the secondary school level. This education lasted for seven years and was divided into two periods. One ran for four years (junior high school) and one for three years (senior high school).

For the four years of junior high school, the subjects taught were Vietnamese, a modern language, history and geography, civics, mathematics, experimental sciences, physics and chemistry, music, physical education (gymnastics or youth activities), handicrafts (carpentry, metal-work, or electrical work) for boys, and home economics (sewing, child care, and cooking) for girls. As far as the modern language was concerned, each student had to choose either French or English as his first foreign language. The total classroom hours were from 25 to

[3] *Education in Vietnam*, D. C. Lavergne and Abul H. K. Sassani, U.S. Department of Health, Education and Welfare, p. 7.

[4] For further details, see *Elementary Education Curriculum*, Department of National Education, Saigon, 1960, pp. 10-15.

27 per week, excluding three hours for gym each week.[5] At the end of the fourth year of junior high school, the student could take a national exam if he wished. If he passed this exam, he was awarded a junior high school certificate.[6] But he was not necessarily required to have this certificate in order to enter senior high school. The junior high school education offered him the essential knowledge to prepare himself for senior high school, which offered a number of more specialized and advanced courses; or if he wished, at the end of junior high school, he could go to a vocational or technical school[7] or go to work.

Upon entering the three-year senior high school, the student had to choose one of four programs of specialized study: Modern Literature, Classical Literature, Mathematics, or Experimental Sciences. These programs were designed to intensify and broaden the learning of the subjects studied in junior high school. Once the program was chosen, the student had to devote more time to a few prescribed courses of study while taking the same subjects he had taken in junior high school, but on a more advanced level and with fewer hours

[5] For further information, see *Secondary Education Curriculum*, Department of National Education, Saigon, 1960, p. 11.

[6] Statistics from 1954 to 1964 showed a very low percentage of passing candidates among those who took this exam. This percentage varied from 18.3 percent to 43.81 percent. For further details, see "Chế Độ Thi Cử" (The Examination System), Huynh Hoa. Mimeographed report presented at the meeting of the National Council of Education, March 30, 1965, p. 27.

[7] This material deals mainly with academic high school education. For further information about the curricula of vocational or technical schools, see *Education in Vietnam*, D. C. Lavergne & Abul H. K. Sassani, U.S. Department of Health, Education and Welfare, pp. 14-15.

each week. All the prescribed courses for each program were required, and there were no elective courses as such since the elective system found in the United States was unknown in Vietnam. Moreover, no matter which of the four programs he chose he had to study a second foreign language. If during his junior high school, he had decided to study French as the first foreign language, then English would automatically become his second foreign language and vice versa. However, the student of Classical Literature had to study Latin or Chinese instead of a second foreign language such as French or English. During the last year of senior high school, all students had to study philosophy. Those students majoring in Classical Literature and Modern Literature had to study it more intensively.[8]

At the end of senior high school, all students had to pass a major examination, given twice every year (one session in June or July, the other in August or September) in order to be awarded the high school diploma or *Tu Tai*. Without this diploma, he was not allowed to register at a college or university. This exam, which lasted for many days, was usually difficult and demanding. Many students failed each year. However, they were allowed to take the exam again and again until they passed. Quite a few students had to repeat it for several years before they passed it. This exam used to be considered a barrier, allowing only the bright and academically able students to continue higher education. Before 1971, this barrier was set up at the end of the second year of senior high school when the *Tu Tai* exams were still composed of two

[8] For more detail, see *Indochinese Refugee Education Guides*, #3, Arlington, Virginia: Center for Applied Linguistics, p. 9; or *Secondary Education Curriculum*, Department of National Education, Saigon, 1960, p. 11.

parts, *Tu Tai* I and *Tu Tai* II. The *Tu Tai* I exam usually ran for many days with a written and an oral test. It was generally very difficult, and only a small percentage of candidates were successful each year. During a period of ten years from 1954 to 1964, this percentage varied from 14.87 to 44.92.[9] If the student passed this exam, he was awarded the *Tu Tai* I certificate and was allowed to finish his high school education by being admitted to the last year of senior high school. He could repeat this exam as many times as he wished until he passed it. Otherwise he could not register for the last year of senior high school. At the end of this year, he had to take another big final exam (written and oral) to get the *Tu Tai* II certificate. Like the *Tu Tai* I exam, this final exam lasted for many days, but was generally considered less difficult than the *Tu Tai* I exam, with a higher percentage of passing candidates, varying from 30.07 percent to 63.70 percent for a period of ten years from 1954 to 1964.[10] These two *Tu Tai* certificates formed his high school or *Tu Tai* diploma. In 1971, the *Tu Tai* I exam was abolished and since then there has been only one overall *Tu Tai* exam at the end of the third year of senior high school.

Students in both public and private schools took the same diploma exams, which were administered by the Department of National Education on the same date throughout the country.

Like France, Vietnam was a diploma-oriented society where a diploma meant better pay, employment, social position, and opportunity for higher education. Too much emphasis was thus placed on obtaining the *Tu Tai* diploma, creating not

[9] See "Chế Độ Thi Cử" (The Examination System), Huynh Hoa. Mimeographed report presented at the meeting of the National Council of Education, Saigon, March 30, 1965, p. 27.

[10] *Ibid.*, p. 27.

only some sort of examination-oriented spirit but also a fear of examinations among high school students. As a result, the ultimate goal of every student was not necessarily getting an education itself but rather being successful in examinations to get diplomas. Although there were regular tests during each school year to decide whether the student met the minimum requirements to go to a higher grade, these tests were generally subjective and administered at long intervals, about every three months or so, by individual teachers without taking into consideration a student's everyday performance. The end result was a lack of concentration on the part of the student during a school year having no major final examinations. He started working hard, usually day and night, only during the last month or two before each such final exam, thus creating a hazardous health condition for himself. American-style objective tests were introduced into the Vietnamese educational system only about one or two years ago, and only to a limited extent. Before that essay-type tests prevailed.

The elective and required subject system, linked to the accumulation of credits, did not exist and was completely unknown in Vietnam; the examination-oriented system or selective system was the Vietnamese tradition. Moreover, extracurricular activities and physical education were not given as much attention as in the United States, while much more weight was placed on "academic" subjects.

Counseling services, a standard feature in American schools, were available only in a very limited number of public schools, but sex education was completely nonexistent. These two domains were generally left entirely to the student and his or her parents.

Finally, high school and primary school curricula were changed on and off in the course of time, but these changes, basically speaking, were minor and only involved technicalities rather than content.

4. Learning Style and Teaching Approach

The traditional way of learning on the part of the Vietnamese student is very likely to be confusing or even disturbing to the American teacher. Likewise, the dynamic and direct approach found in the American educational system will very probably bewilder most Vietnamese students. They might even find the bustle, energy, and informality of the American teacher on the one hand, and the aggressiveness, directness, and competitive spirit of their peers on the other, quite threatening and difficult to understand.

Under the influence of the French culture and educational system, rote learning instead of a problem-solving approach prevailed in Vietnamese schools. Furthermore, team teaching and group work were practically nonexistent, and the student was exposed to learning by observation rather than discovery or experiment. One of the main reasons for this practice was an acute lack of laboratory facilities. Many schools did not have these facilities, especially private schools. Learning by observation, however, might also have something to do with the influence of Taoism, which discourages any disturbance of harmony between man and nature, and scientific experimentation or discovery may lead to this disturbance. It is interesting to note that while Westerners, equipped with the dynamism of Christianity, try not only to analyze nature but also to gain control of it, the Vietnamese, under the influence of Taoism, are taught to adjust or conform to the laws of nature and not to disturb them. Because of this cultural conditioning, too, Vietnamese educators employed the lecture method with a great deal of emphasis on memorization of facts or subject matter instead of encouraging open discussion or critical study. As a result, students had to depend mainly on the teacher's lecture or notes. Very often, after the lecture, the teacher read his notes to the students for them to take home and memorize, thus creating in the students a bad habit of relying heavily on written notes and materials or blackboard illustrations and explanations. Furthermore, the teacher decided practically everything in the classroom, telling the students what to do and how to do it.

More often than not the teacher did not give the students reading assignments beyond class notes or encourage them to read extensively. As a result, Vietnamese students were not accustomed to long and extensive reading or to searching for information on their own. All this left very little opportunity for them to show initiative or develop a critical mind by seeking other sources of information or knowledge. In addition, the majority of Vietnamese students were accustomed to learning through some sort of visual perception and memorization. In other words, they had to see the written form of the lesson even when they learned a foreign language.

In contrast to the American emphasis on independent thought and study with the guidance of the teacher, the traditional Vietnamese education stressed the acceptance of the teacher's authority in the field of his teaching, thus discouraging the questioning of his knowledge. This was clearly a reflection of the profound influence of Confucian teaching, which advocates great respect for learning and knowledge. As a result, respect for the teacher in general was and still is profound.[11] While there is much give-and-take or free exchange

[11] See also p. 10.

of opinions and ideas between the teacher and the student in an American classroom, there was almost no challenge to what was taught in a Vietnamese classroom situation. Criticism of the teacher or questioning of his knowledge was traditionally taboo and practically unknown. As a consequence Vietnamese students, especially female students, are too shy or hesitant to ask the teacher many questions or to express a point of view different from that of the teacher, because they are afraid that doing so might be regarded as a lack of respect for the teacher or might even embarrass the teacher. Students usually did not volunteer the answers unless they were asked to do so, since their cultural heritage taught them to be humble and such an act could be very well interpreted by others as showing off.[12] If they did not understand something or wanted to ask any questions about the lesson, they preferred to ask their classmates outside the classroom, rather than their teachers. Moreover, the students were not accustomed to public speaking or addressing the whole class since they never had an opportunity to practice and were not encouraged by their teachers or classmates. Girl students especially shied away from this type of performance.

In the field of foreign languages, namely French and English, the teacher in Vietnam by and large traditionally used the grammar-translation method and concentrated on reading comprehension rather than employing the audio-lingual method. The development of reading and writing skills was thus a standard feature while less attention was paid to the development of listening and speaking skills. All this was partly due to a lack of qualified teachers of foreign languages and native speakers of these languages whose assistance was much

[12] See p. 35.

needed. Shortage of good textbooks and audio-visual aids worsened the problem. Besides, with a limited number of hours each week varying from three to six hours per language, and having practically no opportunity to practice the languages learned in the classroom, the student could hardly use these languages functionally. Moreover, in relying too much on the grammar approach, the teacher was inclined to spend a lot of time teaching grammar terminology and rules before teaching the student how to make simple sentences or pronounce foreign sounds properly. The result was that most Vietnamese students, on finishing high school, could read and write the two foreign languages better than they could understand or speak them.

Finally, while teamwork and assistance in the classroom among students are common practices in American schools, they were rarely encouraged or even allowed by Vietnamese teachers. In addition to this, Vietnamese students were not accustomed to laboratory work or the use of libraries since these facilities were still considered a novelty in Vietnam and very few students had access to them. The scarcity of textbooks and other learning materials accounted partly for the heavy reliance on the teacher's notes or lectures.

5. Classroom Procedures

In primary schools, one teacher was usually in charge of all subjects for one class throughout the school year. He remained in the same classroom with his pupils day in and day out until the end of the school year. The situation was different in high schools since each teacher could teach only one or two subject matters. At the beginning of each school year, a num-

ber of high school students of the same class or grade varying
from about sixty in public schools to about one hundred or
over in private schools were assigned to a particular classroom,
and they would remain in this classroom throughout the school
year. At the beginning of each school day, they were expected
to be in their assigned classroom to wait for the teacher to
come. At the change of subjects and in contrast to the American practice, they remained in their classroom while the
teacher moved from one classroom to another. When the
teacher stepped in, all students stood up and kept silent to
greet him and at the same time show him respect. They only
sat down when the teacher gave them a signal, either orally
or by a wave of hand, to do so. This type of greeting and
respect was also given to visitors to the class. At first, the
teacher checked the students' attendance and their home assignments at random. Then he proceeded to his lecture for
the day. At the end, he usually read his prepared notes to his
students and gave the same assignments to every student if
such assignments were deemed necessary. In the classroom
they were expected to keep quiet throughout the period so that
work could be done without interference. Talking among students was not allowed and neither was moving around or
changing seats unless the teacher gave permission. By and
large, Vietnamese students were well behaved since discipline
was not only very strict but also strictly enforced. American
teachers would certainly be most delighted to have such well-
disciplined students!

At the end of each period, the students again stood up to
bid farewell to the teacher. Each period usually lasted for
about 50 to 55 minutes with a break of five or ten minutes for
the teacher to move to another class. There was usually a

longer break of about 15 or 20 minutes at the end of the
second period for the students to relax or go to the playground.
Generally speaking, there were no more than five periods
(usually four periods) per day, and school was in session six
days a week.

6. Coeducation and Sex Education

In Vietnam, coeducation was not as common as in the
United States. Wherever it existed boys and girls were still
separated, with girls sitting in the front rows and boys in the
back. Boys and girls never shared the same bench.[13] Furthermore, they were never assigned to the same team in any team
project. This traditional practice derived from an old saying
that males and females should always be separated and mixing
of the sexes avoided.[14] Physical contact between the sexes, at
least in public, was morally unacceptable and might be considered a public offense, while kissing and other shows of
affection between boys and girls in the United States are not
considered out of the way. Naturally, friendships developed
between boys and girls but usually on a reserved basis and
under the watchful eyes of school officials or parents.

While sex education has become a common feature in
American schools, it did not exist and was taboo in Vietnamese
schools. Nobody would have dared to touch such a "shocking"
subject. Traditionally, sex matters were either handled by the
parents or were left entirely to the young people to find out
for themselves. This practice was worsened by the unavail-
ability of sex education materials or counseling services.

---

[13] Long benches were used in classrooms in Vietnam. Each bench
could seat from three to four pupils.
[14] See pp. 45-47.

The reluctance on the part of the Vietnamese to talk about sex probably derives from Confucian influence on Vietnamese culture for many centuries. This reserved attitude about the exposure of the human body or direct reference to any part of the body hidden under clothes is deeply ingrained in the Vietnamese people and should be considered *an extremely delicate topic*.[15]

Therefore, it is of utmost importance that parents should be consulted before any attempt is made to introduce Vietnamese children to any form of sex education, and if such exposure is deemed necessary, it should only be done in a very delicate and tactful way and only when boys and girls are separated.

Furthermore, because of the traditional cultural conditioning mentioned above, the Vietnamese as a whole are not accustomed to exposure, in public or in front of others, of their bodies or of any parts of their bodies from their necks down. As a result, completely acceptable practices in American schools such as group showering, locker room practice, or changing dress in the presence of others will surely be shocking and embarrassing to the Vietnamese. They will undoubtedly show reluctance, if not strong resistance to these practices.

7. The Teacher

The Vietnamese teacher traditionally enjoyed great respect not only from his students but from everybody, including the students' parents. This derived from the traditional profound

[15] *A Handbook For Teachers of Vietnamese Students* (Hints for Dealing with Cultural Differences in Schools), Duong Thanh Binh, Center for Applied Linguistics, Arlington, Va., 1975, p. 21.

respect for learning and knowledge that the teacher was considered to symbolize.[16]

In the classroom he decided practically everything for his students and had almost absolute authority in his teaching and in dealing with his students. His knowledge and teaching approach were never challenged. He was traditionally considered the "spiritual father" and supposed to set a good example for others, especially his students.

The teacher did not have office hours and had practically no contacts with the students outside the classroom or with their parents. His general attitude was that of noncommitment except in the subjects and classes he taught.

Most public school teachers were trained in Teachers Training Colleges with Normal Schools for primary school teachers and Faculties of Pedagogy for high school teachers. All these colleges were administered by the Department of Education, and admission was by very competitive entrance examinations. The training varied from two to four years, and upon graduation the students were appointed to various schools all over the country as civil servants. Because of the serious shortage of graduates from Teachers Training Colleges, other teachers without formal training from these colleges were also hired by the Department of Education to teach at public schools to meet the rapidly increased enrollment demands. These teachers, however, had to meet certain requirements set up by the Department and were generally paid less than the ones with formal training. Similarly, private school teachers generally did not receive formal training from Teachers Training Colleges. They had to get a teaching license from the Department of Education before they were allowed to teach. Requirements

[16] See also pp. 16 and 72.

for a private school teacher's license were by and large lower than those for public schools. Public school teachers were also allowed to teach a limited number of hours each week in private schools. This practice had a two-fold purpose: to ease the shortage of teachers and at the same time raise the standard of private schools. Of course, public school teachers with better qualifications than private school teachers enjoyed much more prestige and respect, not to mention better monetary compensation, than the latter.

8. The Parents

The traditional attitude of parents toward the teacher was always that of respect. In Vietnamese culture, parents rarely or never questioned the knowledge of the teacher. Generally speaking, not only did the parents hold education and learning in high esteem, but they viewed them as the best tool to provide their children with better opportunity for social advancement. They thus usually had strong feelings about the education of their children and were understandably ready to make sacrifices for it.

Educated parents tended to spend a lot more time and money helping their child with his study either by themselves at home or by private tutoring, and as a rule were more concerned with their child's education than were less educated parents. Parents of less or no education usually put their child at the mercy of the teachers and school administrators without giving him any help with his study at home, because of their academic and economic limitations. But generally speaking, Vietnamese parents did teach their children at home in the evening.

Parents in Vietnam usually did not have any contact with the school administrators or the teachers unless there were problems related to their children's education. The teacher usually did not know the parents of his students since the relationship between him and his students' parents was practically nonexistent.

Vietnamese parents traditionally did not actively participate in the activities of the school and did not have any say in the decision-making process or functioning of the school. Although there were a few Parents' Associations in some public schools, not Parent-Teacher Associations as in the United States, these Parents' Associations were not very active. They generally existed in name and acted mainly in an advisory capacity without any real authority. They were usually convened to discuss unimportant issues such as sports matches with other schools, cultural activities, and sometimes disciplinary measures. Even so, attendance at these meetings was minimal. All other important issues, such as the choice of textbooks, hiring of teachers, expansion of school facilities, etc., were either decided by the Department of Education or by the schools concerned. Vietnamese teachers and school officials therefore had much more freedom and authority than their American counterparts in running their school and in dealing with the students and their parents.

9. *Grading, Weights and Measures, Signs and Symbols*

One of the vestiges of the long French presence in Vietnam is the use of the French numerical grading and metric systems.

The numerical grades vary from zero to 20 points with the average or passing grade of ten points. The teacher rarely gives more than 18 points and the lowest grade which can go down as far as zero is not uncommon. Number of points is given out of 20: 12/20 (12 points), 6/20 (6 points), etc. The following is a rough comparison between the American letter grading system and the Vietnamese numerical grading system:

AMERICAN		VIETNAMESE *out of 20*
A+	equivalent to	18-17
A	"	17-16
A−	"	16-15
B+	"	15-14
B	"	14-13
B−	"	13-12
C+	"	11-10
C	"	10- 9
C−	"	9- 8
D+	"	8- 7
D	"	7- 6
D−	"	6- 5
F	"	4 down

The system of weights and measures used in Vietnam is the French kilogram-liter-meter system with grams, kilograms, liters, meters, and kilometers instead of the American pound-pint-foot system with ounces, pounds, pints, quarters, gallons, inches, feet, and yards. Vietnam uses the centigrade temperature scale instead of the Fahrenheit scale. It can be seen that the American system of weights and measures as well as the Fahrenheit scale can be very confusing to Vietnamese.

Finally, the same signs and symbols may mean different things in Vietnam and in the United States. For example:

SIGNS and SYMBOLS	VIETNAMESE	AMERICAN
2/7/1976	July 2, 1976	February 7, 1976
Seven	7	7
Period	2.000 (point after the thousand)	0.40 (decimal point)
Comma	0,40 (decimal comma)	2,000 (comma after the thousand)
Dollar sign	20$00 (piasters)	$20.00 (dollars)
Division	$300 : 12 = 25$	$300 \div 12 = 25$

```
300 | 12
060 | 25
  0 |
```

```
        25
12 | 300
     24
     60
     60
```

10. Adjustment Problems

Upon entering American schools, Vietnamese students will have tremendous difficulty adjusting themselves to a totally new and strange system and environment. Frustration on the part of both the American teacher and his Vietnamese students should not come as a surprise.

Because of the fact that Vietnamese students were accustomed to heavy dependence on the teacher in their learning process, the American teacher may find them passive, unmotivated, lazy, or lacking in creativity and enthusiastic participation in the classroom. If that is so, the language barrier also plays an important part. In other words, if Vietnamese students do not come up to the American teacher's expectations, it might very well be because they do not fully understand English, and therefore do not know what is going on. Moreover, different approaches used by different teachers in this culturally pluralistic society will make them even more confused and add to their existing frustration. This type of problem will be even more serious and acute in urban areas, where there is a diversity of ethnic groups with different cultural backgrounds, whereas in rural areas the approach is more clear-cut and homogeneous.

In addition, the informality, directness, and social behavior of their peers, completely acceptable in American society, will very likely bewilder Vietnamese students. They will find the teacher's informality and lack of authority and respect from the students quite shocking, disappointing, and hard to accept, since they expect the teacher to be much more authoritarian, formal, and respected.

Finally, they will find practically everything around them strange and different from what they were accustomed to: from the language spoken to the signs, symbols, weights and measures; from the classroom set-up to the textbooks, from the learning style to the practices and behavior, and more. In other words, anything they come across in their new country that they were never exposed to at home will create a puzzle if not a problem for them.

It is clear that the adjustment problems facing Vietnamese students will not be easy ones.

V

From the Past to the Future

Now that the traditional values and typical characteristics of the Vietnamese people have been examined in a general way, many questions remain about the changes affecting the Vietnamese man, his family, and his society. Vietnamese values and characteristics changed gradually during peacetime and dramatically during wartime. Even the most deeply ingrained values have not been unaffected by this change, which engulfed people from all walks of life.

The more traditional a Vietnamese, the less he is affected by such change; the less traditional he is, the more vulnerable he becomes. Recent history has witnessed the dramatic impact of forces which have shaken up the traditional Vietnamese culture and its institutionalized values, eroding the foundations of family and of society—such forces as the new materialistic values imported from outside; the constant political upheavals and instability of recent years; widespread corruption; the disruption of normal life and frequent massive displacement of farmers and urban residents during the long and devastating war years.

It is not surprising that we have seen more than a few

young unmarried people deserting their families, something rare even as recently as twenty years ago. Husbands have deserted their wives and abandoned their children to avoid responsibilities. Youngsters have been attracted to materialistic lures, jeopardizing the moral codes that their parents and grandparents had worked so hard to preserve and nurture. Some young girls or wives had to resort to prostitution in order to be able to feed themselves and their loved ones. People seemed to treasure money above everything; loyalty and other spiritual values received only lip service as friends cheated friends and students betrayed teachers. Dignity was ignored for immediate material gains, and filial piety was considered old fashioned. There were many, many heartbreaking scenes.

Despite these saddening developments, there was also an improvement in the quality of life for a great many Vietnamese during the last thirty years: a higher standard of living, better education, increased social mobility. For one thing, more people had access to higher education, thus giving them better opportunity and more mobility. For another, women gradually attained a higher status in society and have had an opportunity to play a more and more important role outside their homes. The number of career women increased rapidly and steadily, even though it remains small in proportion to the total work force. Numerous married women suddenly found themselves without husbands because of the war. They were forced to become self-sufficient and to find one way or another to take care of their fatherless children. As a consequence, women have become more independent, at least economically, because of their new responsibilities and education.

The Vietnamese man has been caught between opposing forces, still imbued with a strong desire to restore and maintain the old traditions and values. He has been fighting a fierce battle within himself. He might find himself helpless in face of the new values fighting to replace the old ones. He might have to accept without much resistance the fact that old customs give way to new demands of life and reality, and that his family is constantly affected by change.

As far as the new Vietnamese immigrants are concerned—as in other immigrant groups—the older generation will find it very difficult to adapt themselves to a new life which is basically alien to them. For the younger generation, the adjustment process will predictably go smoothly and speedily. However, the fading of the old, traditional forces, as well as youthful acceptance of new realities, will undoubtedly widen the gap already existing between the two generations. But the Vietnamese are an able people, noted for their adaptability; they will surely be able to make the best of whatever situation they might find themselves in, given enough time.

Now that the Vietnamese immigrants have been in the United States for a year, reports indicate that although they have been resettled quietly in various parts of the country, they are all still fighting five difficult problems: unemployment, weather, loneliness, the language barrier, and adjustment to a new culture.

Many are holding jobs below their skills, with the national wage averaging $2.50 per hour. It is not uncommon to find former high-ranking officials of the Saigon government, or intellectuals, who now feed their families by working as cleaners or janitors. Some upper-class women who, in Vietnam, never had to step into the kitchen, are now doing what was once reserved strictly for their maids or servants.

For the illiterate, the less educated, and for laborers, this country seems to offer better opportunities for education, employment, and a relatively high standard of living. But it does not necessarily follow that these people can easily adjust to their new way of life. On the contrary, because of their particular background, special efforts and much patience are needed to achieve better results, and frustration on the part of their sponsors or people working with them is to be expected. To help these people make a smooth resettlement may be one of the hardest tasks for their American sponsors. Despite the limited availability of jobs the educated or middle-class Vietnamese think twice or even longer about doing what seems to be menial work, while the illiterate or the laborer will be glad to accept whatever is offered them. For many of the former, a job below their dignity is unacceptable.[1] It does not matter how badly they need it. They might adamantly reject an offer of a janitor's job, but they might accept the same job if the title were not that of a janitor or superintendent but perhaps that of building supervisor or something similar. For them the title or "prestige" is very important to "save face" and definitely plays a role in any of their decisions.[2] They may prefer a job with less pay but with a good title to one with better pay and a "bad" title. It should also be remembered that the training and job experience of a Vietnamese in an underdeveloped economy like that of South Vietnam hardly prepared him for the job market of one of the most sophisticated and developed economies in the world. Most of them, therefore, need either retraining or fresh vocational training in order to get decent jobs. The fact that the Vietnamese came at the time when large-scale unemployment was prevalent in the United States

[1] See p. 36.
[2] See pp. 15 ff.

has added not only to their own frustration but also to that of their willing sponsors.

The weather in the United States is another source of frustration. Vietnamese refugees have been very concerned with the chilling winters, coming as they do from a tropical country where the average temperature is about 90° Fahrenheit and where 100° is not rare. Cold weather has forced many of them to stay home, thus keeping them from school or from conducting business, and slowing down the resettlement process. It has been reported that Vietnamese refugees brought to areas where winters are very cold have begun to move to warmer places such as Florida, California, Texas, etc., to the disappointment of their sponsors and those who have worked hard to help them.

Of course, loneliness and homesickness have also affected the people emotionally. The majority still have relatives and friends in Vietnam from whom they have not heard since their arrival in the United States due to the lack of postal service between this country and Vietnam. They have been very worried about their loved ones, especially those who collaborated closely with the Americans and the old Saigon regime; no one knows what has happened to these people. The emotional problem is even worse for those who left Vietnam in a great hurry at the sudden collapse of the Saigon regime, leaving their spouses and/or children behind.

Of the children who come to this country without relatives or friends, quite a few are troublesome cases for resettlement workers and American sponsors; the absence of their parents or relatives makes the situation more difficult.

In Vietnam traditional values have deep roots. When the heavy winds blow, reeds bend, but when the winds cease, they once again stand straight and tall. In the United States, however, the older generation of Vietnamese immigrants are like mature plants uprooted for transplanting. Whether or not they survive in the new soil depends on the care they receive.

There have been indications that a number of refugees have been unable to cope with their day-to-day problems to a degree whereby they have had serious mental breakdowns or have even attempted to take their lives. Psychiatry was only introduced to Vietnam recently, and there were not many known psychiatrists in South Vietnam, let alone among the refugees. Psychiatric treatment, even if available in the United States, is less efficient, even frustrating, because of the language barrier and the fact that Vietnamese do not like to talk to strangers about their problems. In cases like these, it is useful to seek help from an elderly Vietnamese who can speak English well enough to act as an interpreter. It is even better if this person is a relative or a close friend of the patient. Since Vietnamese show respect for elderly people, they feel more comfortable and are likely to talk easily in such situations.

English itself has been one of the major obstacles in the refugees' resettlement process, and it will remain so for a long time, especially for those middle-aged or older. For Vietnamese, English is a difficult language to learn. Many sounds or structures that Americans take for granted are almost impossibly trying for Vietnamese learners. The resettlement process will never be completely successful until this formidable barrier is overcome.

Adjustment problems for the new immigrants are obviously numerous and complicated. They will remain critical for many years to come if there are no well-coordinated and well-planned efforts on a national scale and on a long-term basis, with the active participation of the Vietnamese themselves.

Let us hope that with good will and adequate preparation these efforts will be made and that the Vietnamese, like so many immigrants who came before them, will one day achieve the adjustment to a new life that we all wish to see.

Bibliography

A *Guide to Two Cultures American and Indochinese.* Inter-agency Task Force on Indochina Refugees. Washington, D.C. 1975.

Duong Thanh Binh. *A Handbook for Teachers of Vietnamese Students: Hints for Dealing with Cultural Differences in Schools.* Arlington, Virginia: Center for Applied Linguistics. 1975.

Duong Thieu Tong. *A Proposal for the Comprehensive Secondary School Curriculum in Vietnam.* Dissertation. Teachers' College, Columbia University. 1968.

Education in Vietnam: Fundamental Principles and Curricula. Arlington, Virginia: Center for Applied Linguistics. 1975.

Elementary Education Curriculum. Department of National Education, Saigon. 1960.

Huynh Hoa. *Chế Độ Thi Cử* (The Examination System). Mimeograph Report Presented at the Meeting of the National Council of Education, March, 1965.

Indochinese Refugee Education Guides. Arlington, Virginia: Center for Applied Linguistics. 1975.

Lavergne, D. C. and Abul H. K. Sassani. *Education in Vietnam.* Washington, D.C.: U.S. Department of Health, Education and Welfare.

Nguyen Dinh Hoa (ed.) *Some Aspects of Vietnamese Culture.* Carbondale, Illinois; Southern Illinois University.

Nguyen Dinh Hoan. *Education in Free Vietnam: An Informative Source for the Evaluation of Vietnamese Students' Credentials.* Project Report. Teachers' College. Columbia University. 1963.

Secondary Education Curriculum. Department of National Education, Saigon. 1960.

Teaching English Pronunciation to Vietnamese. Arlington, Virginia: Center for Applied Linguistics. 1975.

Vuong Gia Thuy. *Vietnamese in a Nutshell.* Montclair, N.J.: Institute for Language Study, 1975.